FOOL'S JOURNEY

First published in 2021
by PANICHELLI

The right of Paul Nelson to be identified as the author of this work
has been asserted in accordance with the Copyright, Designs and
Patents Act 1988

British Library Cataloguing-in-Publication data
A catalogue record for this book is available from the British Library

ISBN: 978-1-5272-9392-2

Every effort has been made to trace the copyright holders and obtain
permission to reproduce this material.

Designed and typeset by
Carnegie Scotforth Book Production

Printed and bound by Severn

In loving memory of my parents,
Sheila and Michael Nelson.

Contents

Introduction

Two so-called "Great Commandments" are at the heart of the teaching of Jesus. They are a succinct summary of the long Jewish tradition from which he came. They may be found in the New Testament in slightly differing versions, at Matthew 22: 35–40, Mark 12: 28–34 and Luke 10: 25–28.

The sayings are about the all-importance of love: for God and for one another. "Do this" Jesus says in the Luke version, "and you will live."

What follows is a ramble round Mark's account of this teaching, stopping off in twenty places: twenty "stations", as it were. Some of the stopping-places may seem a bit random.

Obviously this is not a commentary on the Biblical text. Scholars illuminate scripture through hard-won expertise. I am not equipped to do that.

But I have moseyed round the "Great Commandments" because they have underpinned my life. For the same reason I've woven in some autobiographical material.

ONE

One of the scribes came near...

We don't ask to be born.

We wake up somewhere unknown, among strangers on whom we depend for everything. Gradually we recognize who's friendly and begin to understand their communications.

And as we get acclimatized to this environment and its ways, eventually a time comes when we wonder: Who am I? What am I doing here?

Early on I discovered I was cack-handed and clumsy at most practical tasks...hence probably unemployable in any useful trade or profession. I was, however, curious and studious. And the family into which I was born had a religious aspect: I soon found "God-bothering" came naturally (more on that shortly).

In a seldom-visited part of the Bible called Ecclesiasticus, or the Wisdom of Jesus ben Sirach,[1] we read: "How different" (i.e. from people with useful life-skills) "the one who devotes himself to the study of the law of the Most High! He seeks out the wisdom of all the ancients, and is concerned with prophecies; he preserves the sayings of the famous and penetrates the subtleties of parables; he seeks out the hidden meanings of proverbs...He sets his heart

---

1 (In some parts of the Christian world this is considered one of the Apocryphal or Deuterocanonical books).

on rising early to seek the Lord who made him, and to petition the Most High; he opens his mouth in prayer and asks pardon for his sins."(Sirach 38:34b, 39:1–3a, 5)

That has hardly been a "contemporary" lifestyle during my time on earth, at least not in the places I've lived. However, there have been a few corners where it's still been possible to practise those somewhat "niche" activities.

In ancient Palestine and Judaea, such individuals were known as scribes. They were probably not much use if you needed your gutter fixing...but on the other hand, as the designation suggests, they had learnt to read and write. Their heads were filled with knowledge about what other God-botherers had written in times past. So, like members of priestly castes throughout the world, they were able to affect a certain swagger.

That was less the case, by the time I came along.

However, if your inner vocation propels you in a particular direction, you have to find a way of responding.

Mine was to seek ordination as an Anglican priest. I went on to serve in the role for over thirty years.

At the centre of that ministry were certain words attributed to Jesus Christ, among them the so-called "Great Commandments" about loving God and loving others. Those had first been uttered, according to the Gospel writers, in a conversation between Jesus and a friendly scribe.

For most of my adult life, I have been a religious professional, i.e. a scribe: just one of the common sort, not a figure of authority let alone any kind of theologian. From time to time I've searched out the wisdom of the ancients, occasionally even tried to fathom the subtleties of parables. I claim no expertise in those matters.

However, the two "Great Commandments" of Jesus have been foundational in my life. I was made to learn them by heart as a child. They have always impressed me, even when I tried to ignore them. I picture them like mighty stone monuments from the past, standing there in all weathers; but I also feel them somehow in my blood, as though long ago I had been injected with them.

To live really and truly by such a teaching, day in day out, you would need to be a saint or rishi or bodhisattva. But imagine the joy of that! You would have cracked the code, not only to your existence, to existence generally. You would be not only free, but truly and fully alive.

Or would you? Was I indoctrinated into an illusion all those years ago?

Are Jesus' "Great Commandments" true wisdom to live by? Or are they the impossible decrees of a non-existent deity?

Or is this teaching like some Neolithic stone circle, impressive but irrelevant to us?

I have long wanted to re-explore Jesus' words. I wondered about composing twenty "meditations" or "reflections" (that's the kind of pious activity elderly scribes do towards the end of their careers).

I've gone around dressed up as a priest and spoken from pulpits much of my adult life. It's been an extraordinary assignment, which I've tried to fulfil with genuineness.

However, that's not (quite) what I'll be doing here.

What I want to find out is: what sense (if any) can I make of these famous, revered teachings... just as me? Not as a scribe, not as a member of some priestly caste, not in the name of any church or official organization.

Just as me, fallible, ignorant me, here, now, in England.

The Fool is a Tarot symbol, usually numbered zero. He is said to be the ancestor of the Joker in modern playing cards. The Fool is shown blithely moseying along a cliff-edge, with a silly grin on his face and a little dog for company.

I am moseying round the "Great Commandments" now, not as some reverend priest charged with imparting authorized wisdom, but rather as The Fool might do ("no fool like an old fool," the saying goes). A few stories will get woven in among my pseudo-metaphysical ramblings: like the little dog, yapping away to no-one.

In that weirdest of all Christian scriptures the Book of Revelation, Jesus supposedly says: "To everyone who conquers I will give some of the hidden manna, and I will give a white stone, and on the white stone is written a new name that no-one knows except the one who receives it" (Revelation 2:17).

The point of moseying round such teachings as the "Great Commandments" is not to fill our heads with esoteric information, but to wonder (again), "Who am I? What I am supposed to be doing here?"

The "white stone" Jesus offers is none other than your authentic personhood and unique connection with God.

It can be, to put it mildly, a struggle to discover that.

TWO

...and heard them disputing

"One of the scribes came near and heard them disputing with one another, and seeing that he answered them well, he asked him, 'Which commandment is the first of all?' Jesus answered, 'The first is, Hear, O Israel: the Lord our God, the Lord is one; you shall love the Lord your God with all your heart, and with all your soul, and with all your mind, and with all your strength. The second is this, You shall love your neighbour as yourself. There is no other commandment greater than these'"(Mark 12:28–31).

Ancient scriptures, disputations long ago in a world far removed from mine, let alone yours. Words, beliefs, concepts that may appear to have little connection with the life you, whoever you are, presently inhabit.

They are supposedly at the centre of Christian practice; though being hard, problematic, they've often been ignored in reality.

"Love the Lord your God". For me, it always had to do with love.

I was born in the middle of the twentieth century, not long after the end of the Second World War. Near where we lived, in London, there were "bomb sites", overgrown ruined houses, some with curtains still eerily flapping from empty windows. Even to my childish eyes, certain of the adults around us appeared seriously damaged. An old man used to plod past our house, pushing a pramload of rubbish. "It's all fuckin' shit" he would mutter. One day, I asked Mum what his words meant, and got a shocked wallop round the ear by way of an answer.

Every Sunday Mum and her sister used to go off in an agitated cloud of perfume to a mysterious place. One day they decided to take me with them. I had no idea where the mysterious place was, or what would happen when we got there, though I soon discovered it was a place called Church we were going to, and we would not be swinging on gates, as for some reason I had fondly imagined.

Inside Church were trays of candles giving off a sweetish warmth, and there were many people crammed in, dressed in black, and two enormous brightly coloured statues: Jesus in a red robe pointing at his heart, and Mary in blue looking happy and standing on a snake. In between the statues was a special place where an elderly man in fancy clothes murmured rapidly, his bald head bobbing up and down, accompanied at times by bells jingled by the boys who assisted him. This was called Mass. Most of it was in a language unknown to me. The middle part was quiet, just the man whispering, little bells occasionally tinkling, and people kneeling on the hard boards, coughing, muttering, fingering beads.

I had no idea what was supposed to be happening, but it was clearly something important. Many years later I experienced comparable ignorance and awe in a Buddhist monastery in China. I turned to Mum, that first time, when Mass had finished, and said "I enjoyed that." She stopped dead in her tracks, and looked down at me, aghast, mystified. "You *enjoyed* it? You *are* a funny little boy."

If it were possible to time-travel back to that place and see it through experienced eyes, my guess is it might all look pretty shoddy now, even to me. But what I seem to have picked up on was a sense of presence. Those faithful, mainly Irish people, that priest, believed Christ, and therefore God, the very foundation of the cosmos, became really and truly present in their backstreet chapel as a result of their mumbled enactment of an ancient ceremony. That was the point of it, the reason for being there: to pay homage to "I Am". They wouldn't have expressed it that way, of course.

There was another activity, or inactivity, which occasionally happened at the Church, and it went by the name of Exposition. In the special place between the two statues was sometimes displayed on a pedestal, for a limited time, a round golden object with rays radiating from it, like a golden sun, in the middle of which was a circle of white. This circle of white was the Host, a wafer over which consecratory words and actions of the Mass had been performed. This Blessed Sacrament, as it was always called, was believed somehow to embody the actual, real presence of Christ, and therefore of God, wellspring of all of creation. Here was truly "Immanuel", "God with us," "I Am" displayed on a pedestal in a plain chapel a few yards from a busy street.

What people did was, they sat or knelt there and looked at it. Maybe they said their rosaries, prayers recited silently while fingering beads. But nothing happened; there was no ceremony of any kind. It was called "adoring the Blessed Sacrament." The point was, as you gazed and gazed at the circle of white, believing it to contain Christ, you were gradually drawn in to what felt like an extraordinary mystery; and you might begin to feel as if you yourself were the one being observed. That was sometimes my experience.

There was something about the whole process that might be described as indoor sunbathing. I later learnt that the golden container called a monstrance, with its radiating sun-rays, had been derived from sun-worship practices observed by conquistadores in southern America. I as a young child was initiated into believing that a circle of white bread could contain and focus divine presence: and I sat and gazed on that mystery and was absorbed and fascinated by it. Had I been born into an Aztec civilisation, I might have gazed at whatever sun-worshipping rituals took place and been similarly absorbed. Either way, my heart might have been engaged through such "adoration."

But even in that time and place, our activities were fringe. We were Catholics, a minority in England, tolerated but discriminated against. The world around us, post Second World War, was busy coming back to life; and the Catholic compound within which I endured my schooldays seemed, by comparison with the big world down the road, crusted, fearful, sclerotic. I was happy when the time came to walk out of those narrow gates and never return, to be "condemned to freedom".[2]

And yet. Something had dawned on me, uninvited and yet undeniable. The something happened to be contained within baroque Italianate religious practices; yet it was other than them, elusive of its human bearers. I was helped in glimpsing this by the offhand, disillusioned manner of some of the old male clergy. They used to rattle roughly through Latin Mass as quickly as they decently could... yet presence, the infinitely wondrous I Am, still remained.

Much later, after I'd walked away, temporarily as it turned out, from explicit Christian practice, I was still haunted, allured, stalked by what seemed this unfath-

---

2   Jean-Paul Sartre, trs.Philip Mairet, from the lecture Existentialism is a Humanism, 1946.

omable presence...in noonday sunlight shimmering on the Thames near where we lived, in a pink moon rising over the sea. I once saw an assortment of random hikers and day-trippers sitting in complete silence on a grassy slope, gazing over a valley, and it was much as I remembered Exposition: same atmosphere, same silence. Same wonder.

Back in 1901, American philosopher William James wrote that "there is *something wrong about us* as we naturally stand. The solution is a sense that *we are saved from the wrongness* by making proper connection with the higher powers."[3] Addressing a Christian audience, he was arguing that this was something about which religious men and women in his time might broadly agree, though they might dispute almost everything else. Using Christian language appropriate to his original hearers, he went on to say: "We and God have business with each other; and in opening ourselves to his influence our deepest destiny is fulfilled."[4] That came at the end of a long series of lectures in which he had set out his understanding of certain experiences described by people of his own time.

For me, the all-important word in the two sentences I have quoted from what he wrote is: "connection."

Connection with what?

I have mentioned a sense of presence I became aware of as a small child. The alleged presence of Christ in the sacrament made no demands, except openness to possibility. The sacrament was just there. You looked at it...that was all...and you might feel better for doing so. Of

---

3   William James, *The Varieties of Religious Experience*, Gifford Lectures 1901–2, Fontana edition 1960 p.484

4   (ibid.p.491)

course, someone else could say, "that's just a piece of bread stuck on a pole in a sun-shaped canister," and they'd be sort-of right. Except for the word "just."

All my life I've been surrounded by a supposedly-intelligent default position of scepticism. "Nothing but."

Oh, that's just indoctrination. Nothing but superstitious mumbo-jumbo.

As we, little Catholic children, sat in front of the blackboard at our infant school, an elderly nun scratched in squeaky chalk words of Jesus for us to learn by heart, while outside the window a big real noisy gritty world of lorries and buses and aeroplanes and trains roared on its way.

Most people around us had given up long ago on "business with God". Unsurprising, after two World Wars. They had more pressing things to do.

I have lived surrounded by a default position of "nothing but": and that's fine. Keeping our left-brain fully charged is vital protection against the ideological traps we humans, with our need for connection, are all too likely to stumble into.

But we also need *wonder*, in both senses of that word.

What the old nun was scratching on the blackboard with her squeaky chalk was, "Jesus said, 'Hear, O Israel: the Lord our God is one Lord; and thou shalt love the Lord thy God with all thy heart, and with all thy soul, and with all thy mind, and with all thy strength. This is the first commandment. And the second is like, namely this, Thou shalt love thy neighbour as thyself. There is no other commandment greater than these."

No other commandment greater. Even if given by a head teacher, a chief executive, or a commanding officer, a president or sovereign, a bishop or mullah, or a boss man or woman. No. These, according to Jesus and St Mark, trump any other orders or instructions we could possibly be given.

The words were and are presented in antiquated form, smoked by the stale miasma of old religion from which people in my lifetime have generally fled. And yet...clear away a little of the old varnish, and there begins to appear an invitation to *wonder*...to *connect*.

With what? And to do so, how?

THREE

Which commandment is the first?

I was once sitting in a bar near to a group of young men who were discussing what they were about to read at university. One, the most talkative, seemed to be about to study theology. I heard him say to his friends, "The trouble with theology is, sooner or later you get back to 'God said.'"

I suppose that's one issue people of my generation had with such religion as was handed down to us. You did, pretty soon, get back to "God said," and some of what God was alleged to have said sounded, to put it mildly, absurd, and to put it more strongly, tyrannical...deeply unattractive. Intelligent well-meaning folk seemed to have gotten roped in as apparatchiks of a bipolar deity.

I can recall listening to a sermon by a priest friend, a jovial fellow who I knew enjoyed a drink or six, and what he told us was that God our almighty Father loves us, wants the best for us, which is the reason for his commandments. If we don't obey his commandments, you see, we will all end up in hell, torment for all eternity.

Knowing my friend's witty, humane persona, I was waiting for him to shed some interpretative light on this psychotic tyranny...but he didn't. That was it.

In particular, the God preached to us when I was a schoolboy had no more than a grudging toleration of sex, under strictly limited licence of marriage and for purposes of procreation only. All other sexual desires or energies were demonic deceptions, most mortal of mortal sins. That didn't prevent some of the staff at my Catholic boys' school seeming obsessed with them. One priest's "religious instruction" classes consisted largely of tirades against the evils of masturbation, which word he would write in huge letters on the blackboard. "Your life with God thrown away for all eternity for a moment of pleasure", he would rant.

Unsurprisingly in the face of such diatribes, "business with God" came to seem laughable really, for me and for many of the people around me. Churches appeared to be places dedicated to keeping us shamed and subservient: unworthy, endlessly-transgressing subjects of a despotic, "perfect" ruler. To walk away and not look back felt, at that time, a sane reaction.

So, as I entered adulthood, supposed divine commandments were not high on my reading list. And nor were the scriptures wherein people found them.

What every Christian church contains, in a place of honour, is the vast dark unimaginably complex book, or rather, compendium of books, called The Bible. This sits, usually, on a stand or lectern near the front. It contains writings from long, long ago, translated into something approximating to common language. Mixed up in it all are what purport to be divine commandments.

Nobody in the world can claim to understand the entire Bible. Some people wrestle with it much of their lives. That's what happens, if some aspect of the Bible resonates: you end up struggling with the whole mighty, perplexing, monstrous beast. Out of that struggle might, or might not, emerge some ongoing wisdom. Quite likely not: you may just end up baffled.

Partly on account of how it has been used for millennia, the Bible is not just any collation of ancient literature: it is, truly, a magic volume, or bundle of volumes. Even after so many years, so many centuries, the Bible can seem organic, alive, unpredictable. It has caused terrible things to happen in history. Out of it, or out of the struggle with it, have come inspirations and paradigm shifts. It is, truly, an astonishing beast. Who knows what it still has in store for us humans? And it sits there silent on the lectern in any church, looking like an innocent part of the furnishings. Until someone opens it and begins to read.

I did not pick up the Bible and start reading because of any longing to reacquaint myself with this oriental bazaar of perplexity, but because of certain experiences I had. It was perhaps a foolhardy thing to do, picking up that mysterious old book and imagining I might understand what was written there.

By far the greater part of the Bible is taken up with Jewish scriptures which Christians refer to as the "Old Testament." The dedicated Christian part, the "New Testament," is appended at the back like an addendum or afterthought. The Jewish scriptures contain (among many other extraordinary writings) 613 commandments or "mitzvoth" some positive ("you shall") and some negative ("you shall not"). The numbers are approximate, and rabbis have argued about their exactitude, as about much else. Some of the mitzvoth might appear to us petty opinions on hairdressing fashion and suchlike (Leviticus 19:27) or the supposed evils of cross-dressing (Deuteronomy 22:5) or eating shellfish (Leviticus 11:11). There is much, as one might expect, concerning sex (e.g. Leviticus 18:22, 19:20) religious ritual (e.g. Leviticus 1:5–9) and what was considered occultism (e.g. Deuteronomy 18:11) But amidst all these legalistic entanglements, suddenly up pops a visionary, generous-hearted pronouncement: "You shall not take vengeance or bear a grudge against any of your people, but you shall love your neighbour as yourself: I am the Lord" (Leviticus 19:18).

This is part of what Jesus was quoting, selectively, in his Gospel conversation with the scribe.

For us humans to live in any kind of social harmony and order, we have to trust our preferred way is proper, righteous and moral. Therefore, one way or another, we generate laws, "commandments."

Unsurprisingly, that has particularly been true of religious practice. Three thousand years ago in India, sacrificial rituals conducted by Brahman priests were thought to be nothing less than the lynchpin of cosmic order (one outcome being "the enormously enhanced prestige of the Brahman priest who alone had the professional knowledge necessary for the scrupulously correct performance of the sacrificial ritual"[5]. Those were the days!)

When I was a little boy, I was roped in as an altar server at our Catholic church; Mass at that time was still recited according to the ancient "Tridentine" formula, involving a lengthy series of Latin responses, spoken by the server, which I had to memorize, as well as elaborate choreography. The priest's all-important role was to perform the actions, gestures and script of Mass *exactly* as prescribed by sacred tradition. No deviations from the authorized stage-directions were allowed. People of female gender were automatically excluded from the "sanctuary" while Mass was going on; and no girl or woman was permitted to touch any sacred paraphernalia, despite there being a flotilla of nuns attached to our church.

Even to my eight year old self it seemed puzzling that I, dodgy smelly little schoolboy, was allowed into the sacred huddle but the nuns, holy as holy could be, were not.

---

5   Trevor Ling, A History of Religion East and West, Macmillan 1968, p.51

The generation of commandments, laws and rituals is part of something we humans have done for a very long time, which is to make sacred texts, scriptures: "God said".

For centuries such compositions were passed on orally; when texts eventually got scratched on parchment, there ensued cyclones of argumentation about their meaning.

Starting as I did from a disenchanted, suspicious view, I was surprised continually by how volatile some of the Bible writings still are, how powerfully they can work within and amongst us, how they still seem capable of being inhabited by the Holy Spirit. I also found that the Bible can be used, and often is, to box in the Spirit: to oppress, to constrain, not to throw a window open to hope but to slam a door in its face.

No wonder, then, that good people are sometimes fearful of the terrible, beguiling old book, and prefer to leave it sleeping on the lectern.

A characteristic of any scripture is that it is from long ago, when people knew nothing of Australia or America, let alone the Great Nebula of Andromeda or black holes or psychotherapy or cyberspace.

But supposing what we imagine as the divine, the beloved, the originating mystery, was to communicate with us now, today, anew...how might that be? What form would such communication take? How might it be described? What might be imparted or shared?

This chapter is supposed to be about "commandments", and I've been expatiating about the Bible and have not yet mentioned the most famous "commandments" in the Jewish scriptures, the so-called Decalogue or Ten Words. These are presented in the Old Testament as the foundation of law and morality itself, given by God to Moses on Mount Sinai amid "thunders and lightnings, and a thick cloud upon the mount, and the voice of the trumpet exceeding loud" (Exodus 19:16). The Ten Words are believed by traditionally-minded Jews and Christians to be the ultimate "God said", out of which the other 613 (or however many) pronouncements were drawn. That is certainly how the Bible as handed down to us presents the story. The Ten Words (Exodus 20:1–17) are given to Moses by God, engraved on two tablets of stone, amid scenes of the utmost awesomeness and drama. Generations of faithful Jewish and Christian people have meditated on that story, and found therein profound and life-changing inner sustenance; and thousands of pilgrims make the arduous journey to Jebel Musa in Egypt, traditional site of the event, there to contemplate the Covenant between heaven and earth of which the Ten Words are the seal.

You may be aware, however, that over recent centuries the Bible has been studied as probably no other book. Scholars of ancient languages, archaeologists, students of history, literature, anthropology, mythology and every other -ology have pored over the texts. They continue to do so; biblical writings are analysed, deconstructed and examined from every angle. Academics submit the hallowed texts to what can seem a pitiless barrage of interrogations.

As I understand it a consensus of present western scholarship would certainly be that the Decalogue so-called is "a comparatively late arrival, probably later than the individual laws in the Covenant and Deuteronomic Codes that were arranged to look as though they are a detailed spelling-out of its implications. The Ten Commandments now appear...as a prologue to the detailed laws, but (like the Foreword to many books, usually written last) they were probably compiled later than those laws."[6]

---

6   John Barton, A History of the Bible, Allen Lane, 2019, p.78

Thus the cinematic marvel of Exodus, with its awesome patriarch descending onto the mountain and presenting humankind with laws written on tablets of stone, does not have to be taken absolutely literally.

And yet... that Exodus story from a dreamtime far removed from my suburban imagination has inspired generations of Jews, Christians and others who have endured cruelty and injustice and tried nonetheless to lead moral lives because, they believed, "God said."

So here's a dilemma: in order to taste the bracing medicine of ancient wisdom, is it obligatory also to swallow antique cosmology along with spoonfuls of fierce and fiery legend?

It used to be taught within Christianity that the first five books of the Bible were the inspired though unaided work of Moses. The psalms were believed to be from first to last songs of King David. The four New Testament gospels were assumed to have been written by eye-witness apostles. Centuries of scholarship have demolished those and other traditional beliefs, and put in their place a picture in which that literature, like everything else, *evolved*. Remembrances, oral passings-on...inspired bursts of composition... editing, rewriting, cutting-and-pasting... political reordering, multitudes of translation, limitless scope for confusion and creativity...and so on.

Yet the Ten Words still seem foundational. They remind us of aspects of our nature we might prefer to gloss over: our rapacious instincts, our envy, our addiction to idolatrous thought-forms. They, the Ten Words, can be a remedy, a signpost, a handle to take hold of, a barrier to kick against.

Such an *evolved* human production may surely be described as: inspired.

That, to me, is how "God said", and still might say:

through sacred texts, yes, but always alongside our living breathing human experience. Power with, not power over. Shining through, not breaking through.

Out of such searching, fresh communication might emerge. No one knows or can know what did or didn't happen in the distant past. The old stories burn their way into our souls; but they are there as warm-up acts for the real business, which is illumination for this present moment, right here, right now.

The "Great Commandments" enunciated by Jesus are, at the very least, highly *evolved* words. We may read them in a book, we may mosey round them and poke at them and hug them as if they were some great stone circle. We are, of course, completely free to ignore them. The point about "God said" is that one of God's names is freedom: look at the world around us, in all its glory and horror and randomness.

FOUR

The first is...

For me, it was always about love. The object of that love, though real, remains elusive. I don't know how it happened, this falling in love with the originating mystery.

I had been born into a family of partly Irish and Italian extraction. Mum used to go to Mass and was a believing Catholic (though fiercely rebellious when it suited). Dad by contrast had grown up in a non-churchgoing Protestant family. His parents had turned to Spiritualism, as many did in the first half of the twentieth century. When I was little, he never accompanied us to church; but he had had to agree, when Mum and Dad married, that any children would be brought up Catholic.

What I can remember Mum doing when I was very little is teaching me simple traditional Christian prayers: Our Father, Hail Mary, Glory Be. If I recite those prayers now, I can still sometimes see in my mind's eye the house we used to live in all those years ago. As far as I can recall, they were happy times, learning those words, and they brought Mum and me close together.

So, how useful is it me telling you any of this? Not very, I guess. It's just to note how traditional faiths, traditional pictures of God and understandings of life used to get handed on. Coercion mixed with love.

The picture I was given was of an invisible family, somehow "above" us, who watched over us, mostly for the good: mysterious, but then so were my flesh and blood relations. I knew pretty much nothing about the lives, let alone the inner thoughts, of my parents, grandparents, aunties and uncles.

They had all survived something to which they referred frequently, "the War". (Shattered remnants, burnt out buildings and crazed people with paramilitary psychoses were all about us).

Both sets of grandparents had also endured something longer ago but equally terrible, spoken of as the Great War, at that time still a vivid memory though overshadowed by the more recent horrors.

From our very earliest days, we are schooled by agendas: received opinion, shared beliefs, propaganda, adverts. What creedal matter have you absorbed while growing up?

In post-war England, where lorries and buses and aeroplanes and trains roared on their way, agendas were mostly materialistic. So a few prayers spun into the mix at least gave me a rumour of other possibilities.

And they, along with the strange goings on at the little church we went to, had the effect of unbolting a trapdoor in my childish imagination. Those ancient words, "Our Father, who art in heaven, hallowed be thy name..." pointed to a reality other than the everyday, yet very close: our Father in heaven could see us, and every night before going to bed I was taught to ask for his protection and blessing on our family and those round about us.

That is what traditional religion used to do, and maybe in some places still does. It unbolts a secret inner trapdoor.

Whatever world we inhabit is likely to remain a closed circle of human needs and ambitions and opinions and beliefs: and however big that circle may grow on account of our cleverness, it will still stay closed, and remain a circle.

The ancient symbol of that is "Ouroboros": it's a picture of a snake eating its tail.

But the innocent prayers I was taught pointed to a possibility that the circle might be transformed into an upward spiral. "You shall see heaven open", Jesus says in St John's gospel, "and the angels of God ascending and descending upon the Son of Man" (John 1:51). That is "the way of the spiral into the infinite."[7]

How might such doorways to wonder be unbolted now?

Transformation does seem to be that for which we humans have infinite capacity.

Even in my childhood, however, let alone yours, not only the "packaging" but the content of traditional faiths seemed sclerotic and antiquated. And I have spent much of my adulthood priming a religious system which has remained of minuscule interest to most of my contemporaries.

I stayed loyal because for me it opened a doorway that led to the originating mystery and to ongoing, transformational love.

"By love may He be getyn and holden; bot bi thought neither:"[8] so said a fourteenth century English priest in a book of spiritual instruction called, wonderfully, the "Cloud of Unknowing." The author was telling his readers: God may not be known or touched or entered into by words or doctrines or argumentation or even by belief, but through attraction, through love.

So it has been for me, and so it will have been for many, within all faiths that have ever existed. Structures

---

7   Anon. (Valentin Tomberg), trans. Robert Powell: Meditations on the Tarot, Tarcher/Penguin, 1985, p.483

8   Anon., The Cloud of Unknowing, ed. Patrick J. Gallacher, Western Michigan University, 1997, p.36

sacred, venerable: but pointing beyond themselves, making it possible for adherents to think thoughts of the sublime, to sunbathe in the radiance of heaven.

At their best, religious systems speak languages of love. They open the circle, if only for half an hour, so that it becomes an upward spiral into light, a pathway to unknowing, to wonder.

And yet...in my lifetime rejecting faith has often felt like rejoining the human race.

My disloyalty to religion had to do with people being expected to carry on thinking and believing in the manner of seven year olds, long after they had become adults.

Christianity, like all the world's major religious traditions, developed at the hands of inspired people, who didn't know about football or Antarctica, let alone jet propulsion or quantum physics or the Great Nebula of Andromeda.

Perhaps above all, they couldn't know about *evolution*.

If we list great discoveries that have come about in the last several hundred years, surely top of the list is evolution. Not only does that concept frame the story we tell of how anything comes to be, but evolution includes every atom and every human activity, no matter how holy. Scriptures evolve. Religious traditions have evolved.

Most importantly, we ourselves evolve. To live is to change. Our innermost being does not remain entirely as it was when we were seven, unless some pathology is forcing that to happen.

Tragically, for all the beauty contained within it, I have often seen religion behave as just such pathology.

When "sacred attraction" is triggered, we may live for a while in a universe of fixed beliefs and simplistic explanations. We might choose to remain indefinitely in such a world, and we might value and treasure the sense of being part of "One True" community or tradition, "Rightly Guided." Such a community will demand stringent and steadfast adherence to its doctrines and practices. No-one would deny the powerful appeal of such sacred belonging, in our fragmented world.

But other-worldly love, once awakened, is always likely sooner or later to endanger supposed orthodoxies. "Where is God?" asked the catechism I was taught at infants' school, and the (unwittingly subversive) answer we chanted back was "God is everywhere." That means God is in the most unexpected places, people and circumstances, not only those deemed appropriate by guardians of Rightly Guided faith.

So questioning, doubt, exploration, argument will naturally unfold. And so will dismay at the state of the world, grief at its injustices and wrongs, passionate anger, maybe raging at that very presence with which connection seemed to have been made. The Old Testament psalms are full of such storming perplexity.

Human souls develop and evolve; they don't remain fixed in a single configuration. They burst out, somewhat as plants stretching for the sun. There isn't, can't be, a point at which that ceases.

The Christian vision in which I was nurtured describes God as "infinite." That means what it says: boundless, unimaginable, not hemmed in by any limitation, human or otherwise.

But the deity as presented in churches I served most often felt very finite indeed, limited and defined by cultures long past: "...it was believed that the original forms of spiritual presentation were somehow cut in stone, never to be changed or improved on again..."[9]

For me, love, once triggered, easily jumped such man-made obstacles. It was like the umbilical cord connecting an infant to its mother. In the gospels, when Jesus performs healings, he often says to the recipient "Your faith has saved you" (e.g. Luke 18:42). He can't be referring to belief in some particular doctrine, or adherence to a creed. It is connection he's meaning: openness to the possibility of being fed, being healed.

Such openness comes about through love, flowing both ways. "By love may He be getn and holdn..."

But how might that love be awakened? Holy places abound, great and celebrated ones, along with tiny shrines and wells, groves and clearings. But we know such things are meaningless to many if not most of those around us. Does that mean original light and connection are unavailable to the majority of the human race?

A niche "deity" ministering only to people like me? That's no God, just an ancient idol.

So...how might you notice connection, if, like most of my contemporaries, you are not "religious"?

I don't know. You are unique.

But here's a suggestion: when in wild nature, or windsurfing or rock-climbing...while making or listening to music...in the process of some act of compassion or shared enterprise...you might suddenly become surrounded by, or alive to, a presence you hadn't experienced before.

Such happenings are sometimes called epiphanies. They're fleeting temporary moments of disclosure. Often they are difficult to understand, and we file them away.

---

9   Ken Wilber, The Religion of Tomorrow, Shambala, 2017, p.15

But other times it's more a case of realizing you are in love.

Such love will be only a beginning, but it can't un-happen once it's happened. You are, allegedly, in touch with the underlying wisdom and purpose of the cosmos.

Only, don't expect clarity or instant understanding. "Thirty spokes on a cartwheel" wrote Lao Tzu. "Go towards the hub that is the centre – but look, there is nothing at the centre and that is precisely why it works!"[10]

Though it has been (what Hindus and Buddhists might call) my dharma to perform religious duty, I am not in any way persuaded only religious practice points to enlightenment...how dreary would that be! The originating mystery I have tried (inadequately) to serve may make itself known in ways entirely beyond my comprehension, but that will be clear and familiar to you.

All I can say is, whatever unfolds, love in some way will be part of it. Without love, as St Paul wrote, "I am a noisy gong, or a clanging cymbal." (I Corinthians 13:1)

(And you know as well as I do that's one thing to say and quite another to understand, let alone do. I'm sitting writing these words with cotton wool stuffed in my ears, because a neighbour in the house next door is playing his music at high volume and singing loudly over the top. I'm not finding it easy to love him, right at this moment).

So what am I supposed to do, and how am I supposed to do it?

---

10 Tao Te Ching, trans. Man-Ho Kwok, Martin Palmer, Jay Ramsay, Element, 1994, p.57

FIVE

The Lord our God (i)

When I was a small boy, manufacturers of breakfast foods sometimes gave away small gifts in their cereal packets, designed in to make people collect more of whatever the something was, and thus purchase more cereal. One such giveaway, sometime in the late 1950s, was of plastic dinosaurs.

A teaspoon-sized Brontosaurus had tumbled out one morning amid the cornflakes. At night when I went to bed, I could see the little creature in my bedroom, its tiny head on a long neck turned so it seemed to be looking back towards me. I remember lying there feeling real love for the little plastic figure, along with a desire to possess others the cereal company was promising: Tyrannosaurus Rex, Stegosaurus, Triceratops.

But having heard in school what we had been told about loving God before all things, I thought: maybe I love this dinosaur more than I love God?

At that moment, that was how it was. It provoked a mini-crisis of conscience.

There would be many more plastic dinosaurs to follow as I grew older. Maybe there are a few more yet to come.

One glaring and immediate problem with identifying love as the key to wisdom is this: much of our human love at best is ignorant, at worst catastrophic. "The heart is deceitful above all things, and desperately wicked" wrote the prophet Jeremiah in the Old Testament (Jeremiah 17:9). "Who can know it?" Who indeed?

Yet what we're thinking about here is not some optional, self-indulgent distraction but the primeval, originating force running through the entire cosmos, as Teilhard de Chardin eloquently described: "...this fundamental vibration...at the basis, or rather at the summit, of every great emotion."[11] That which animates us in our little everyday lives: a tiny domesticated version of "the Love that moves the sun and the other stars."[12]

So: contemplate for a moment the impersonal force of gravity, and dark matter seeming to bind creation together. Picture in your mind clashes of galaxies...collisions of moons...oceans of superheated plasma...the titanic emptiness of interstellar space...

Of course we humans have not been able to imagine such marvels until fairly recently, since the invention of telescopes and development of observational sciences. But now we can glimpse creation in some of its vast force and wonder.

Teilhard is suggesting its brute energy as a primal sacrament, an outward sign of an originating faraway grace (lamely hinted at in the pious phrase "God is Love.").

So think of your own early experiences of love: that which your original family gave you, love of friends, love of animals and places.

And then consider your first erotic or romantic stirrings.

What you are recalling, according to Teilhard, are not just fond, embarrassing or bleak memories but tastes of

---

11 Pierre Teilhard de Chardin, trs. Bernard Wall, The Phenomenon of Man, Fontana, 1965, p.292

12 The last line of Dante's "The Divine Comedy", as I'm sure you know.

the taproot itself...to be welcomed, though needing also to be trained and channelled so they don't overwhelm and wreck everything.

"Seek first the kingdom of God..." Jesus advises (Matthew 6:33). And when asked what really matters, what is "the first commandment of all," he replies, "Love", but not just any sort. "Love the Lord your God."

Now, the culture in which I have lived my adult years would suppose a "fundamentalist" meaning to that statement which would corral us humans back in a closed religious pen where we probably don't want to be. You could read the words that way.

I grew up in an old-fashioned environment in which "the Lord your God" did sometimes suggest the fierce old man thundering "Thou Shalt Not" on the mountaintop. Whom one was supposed to obey, or else.

However, what had caught my attention by the time I was five was not that forbidding figure, nor even the kindly all-seeing invisible Father to whom we Catholics addressed our bedtime prayers.

No, what had begun to prise open the trapdoor in my heart was the presence that came among us whenever Mass was celebrated. The presence was allegedly that of Jesus Christ, somehow part of God and who had "taken flesh" in a faraway country a very long time ago. Images of him smiling in supposedly Galilean robes were everywhere when I was growing up. He would often be pictured pointing to an exposed and bleeding heart.

Those images, however, were just images, people's ideas of what this person might have looked like. The presence was something more than that. It was real.

That, to me, was an object of fascination, and ultimately

of love: more propitious long-term than any passing dinosaur.

OK, that love has got warmed in the telling, as probably with all theophanies.

But at the heart of it is something cataclysmically definite: a strong remembrance of "coming home."

"Where is God?" the catechism teacher at school asked us five year olds. "God is everywhere", we chanted in reply. "What shall it profit a man, if he gain the whole world, and suffer the loss of his soul?"(Mark 8:36) we recited off the blackboard. Our teachers were benign, often elderly nuns. "Out of the depths I have cried unto thee, O Lord", we were taught to pray for those who had died, "Let thine ears be attentive to the voice of my supplication."(Psalm 130:1, 2)

Indoctrinated? Undoubtedly. The world portrayed to us by teachers, clergy, nuns was a church-centric one in which, for example, the myth of Adam and Eve was an actual account of something that had happened in real time. It is hard even for me, let alone you, to imagine, now, the narrowly uncritical manner in which children were spoon-fed Catholic teachings back in the mid-twentieth-century. And as you will probably have heard, the devil and original sin were as omnipresent in this Catholic universe as God.

On the plus side, questions that have troubled humans since consciousness began (why is anything here? who am I? what is this all about?) were being engaged with, and answers given to us children, if only out of the penny catechism... unlike in that busy concrete and brick world outside the school gates, where they would have been dismissed as meaningless. What we were being offered turned out to be a surprisingly generous and flexible template through which to view the visible and the invisible, the profane and the mysterious. Not "consumers," but immortal souls, we were encouraged to love those who hated us and converse with our guardian angels.

Love was spoken of as all-important. It was also shown daily in the demeanour of those who taught.

I am grateful for the "container" those kindly people gave me. I have struggled to find ways of offering something equally generous and inspiring to children I have taught, while leaving out the ingredient we might rightly call fundamentalism.

It has seemed to me children I have worked with over my thirty subsequent years as an Anglican priest have been every bit as indoctrinated as I was, only in materialist, consumer creeds in which the puny supposed agenda has been to climb some achievement-ladder or attain possessions-based ephemeral butterflies of happiness or success.

When I was nine, something incredibly exciting happened, which inspired my love and wonder in a completely new way. Yuri Gagarin flew into space, the first human ever to do so. I was fascinated by space. Gagarin was Russian, and at that time Russia was viewed here in England as the ideological enemy. But the brilliance of Gagarin's achievement melted hostility. A few months after his flight, he came to London, and I was allowed to see him as he passed in an open-topped Rolls Royce on his way back to the airport after visiting the Queen. I was thrilled and amazed to see the man who had done this incredible thing. I was bursting with excitement to talk about it.

Imagine my dismay when my Gran, kindest of people, a woman of benevolence and selflessness who I loved utterly, turned to me and said, "Yes, yes, he's a very brave young man. It seems so sad to think he'll go to hell when he dies."

What? But she was right, according to the literal sense of the Catholic doctrine "Extra Ecclesiam Nulla Salus"[13], which she would have had drummed into her from pulpits over many years. Gran was an utterly gentle woman, who would never have been capable of condemning anyone. The deity of the "One True Church", however, was somewhat more relentless...

At eight, I had become an altar-boy, who assisted the priest at Mass. In order to serve at a simple Low Mass, one had to learn complicated ritual choreography dating from the sixteenth century, along with a magical script of Latin responses: we had to have all this by heart before we were allowed on stage at a real service. As mentioned before, it did not escape my notice that the nuns, living embodiments of sanctity or so it seemed to me, were not allowed near the altar during Mass, while we, dodgy pre-pubescent males, dolled up in ill-fitting cassocks and cottas, bowed and genuflected and rang bells in the Holy of Holies. When I mentioned that one day to Mum, she launched into a vehement tirade about how, when Jesus was on the cross, it was the women who stayed with him to the end: all his male so-called friends ran away. At the time I was shocked by the forcefulness of this response, especially as one of those "so-called friends" was the great St Peter himself, the rock on whom the Catholic Church was supposedly founded.

Serving at High Mass was more complicated than Low Mass choreographically, and involved much business with holy water buckets, torches (candles on long wooden poles), censers full of incense and spitting charcoal, and much bowing and genuflecting in unison up and down steps

---

13 Outside the (Roman Catholic) Church, no salvation.

to the accompaniment of sacred polyphony. Being of the two-left-feet persuasion, I found all this daunting, and was never very good at it. However, I was a willing participant in the ceremonies. My favourite was the lighting of the New Fire, deep in the dark small hours of Easter. At such moments it seemed to me we were surrounded by all who had participated in Mass in times past and all who were doing so now, near or far away. It was as if we were for a short while bound together in love, along with angels and archangels, in a magical place lifted out of normal time where we somehow shared Christ's great work for the world.

That's the specialness of ritual. I still to this day have a sense of the wonder of it, and share Valentin Tomberg's insight that "...one never prays alone...there are always others – above, or in the past on earth – who pray with you in the same sense, in the same spirit or even in the same words. In praying, you always represent a visible or invisible community together with you."[14] (I have often found pagans understand this at least as well as Christians. Josephine McCarthy, for instance, writes: "By walking a path already trodden, contacts and powers woven into that pattern are energized and interacted with. The trodden path becomes a window over the generations until it is like a programme whereby you throw the switch and on it comes.")[15]

In my lifetime American philosopher Ken Wilber has attempted to map our unfolding spiritual "Levels of Consciousness" using a spectrum of rainbow colours. He pictures early-level religion of the sort described here as red

14 Meditations on the Tarot, p.619
15 Josephine McCarthy, Magical Knowledge, Book 1, Mandrake, 2012, p.121

and amber. Red is the colour of the infant ego, "throwing its weight about". You create an imaginary world. You make things happen. However, "Continued interaction... leads the subject to realise that his or her thoughts do not egocentrically control, create or govern the world...Maybe I can't order the world around, but Daddy (or God or the volcano spirit) can."[16]

This is described by Wilber as the amber stage, and "... the focus now is to learn the correct rituals and prayers that will make the gods and goddesses intervene and alter the world for me."[17] Such religion is absolutist. There can only be "One True" whatever.

"Amber" religion (or "Mythic Membership") was something I loved deeply for a while. It loved me back, embraced me utterly, involved me in mystical secrets, whispered to me about God.

Then I shed that skin. Other obsessions kicked in. The taken-for-granted order my pre-modern Catholic tribe imposed on its members seemed easy to abandon amid the fluorescent new world opening up in nineteen-sixties London.

Yet, though I proudly wrote "none" on an opinion poll enquiring about religion, the trapdoor in my heart had been well and truly unbolted. I sought presence in other ways, in secret tree-places, by the Thames shore, amongst the stars. I sought transcendence through music. And needless to say, I sought love. Who doesn't?

And sometimes I deliberately ignored the open doors of churches, or bells calling across the fields.

---

16 Ken Wilber, Sex, Ecology and Spirituality, Shambala, 1995, p.227
17 Ibid., p.227

Ken Wilber writes: "...just as when climbing a real ladder, the climber... loses the view from the previous rung – but the previous rung itself remains in existence...development is 'transcend and include,' or 'negate and preserve'... successive Views...are negated and transcended (as the self steps up to a new and higher rung and its View), but the structure-rungs themselves are included and preserved (all rungs remain in existence)."[18]

Love is what wakes us to climb or grow in the first place...as the honeysuckle plant in my garden does, reaching for the sun. I'm grateful to the women and men of the "One True Church" who supplied early rungs that opened up a view, and a "...strong container to hold the contents and contradictions that arrive later in life."[19]

But, as I evolved into adulthood, traditional church was obviously not going to provide encouragement to seek further, or at all. "Will there be" asked Ken Wilber a few years later "a conveyor belt that individuals can safely ride from pre-rational to rational to transrational floors, or will religion remain merely the repository of humanity's childhood?"[20]

As you will by now have noticed, I am interweaving this exploration of Jesus' "Two Great Commandments" with a few reminiscences. The reason is not to make out my particular path has been special – I've lived a fortunate life in the privileged west – but to try to show the larger idea: primeval love awakening us small humans, as the sun draws out plants and trees.

---

18 Ken Wilber, The Religion of Tomorrow, Shambala, 2017, p.187
19 Richard Rohr, Falling Upward, Jossey-Bass, 2011, pp.25/26
20 Ken Wilber, Integral Spirituality, Integral Books, 2006, p.200

As is obvious, there are infinite numbers of paths, not all equally helpful.

Yet truth is truth...here and on whatever channels, wavelengths and frequencies may be, among the remotest galaxies.

That's what I'm hoping to explore further in what follows.

SIX

Jesus answered...

But first, a few words about Jesus Christ, master of the spiritual stream into which I was immersed and within which I have continued to be both nurtured and baffled, sometimes simultaneously.

Part of the fascination of Jesus of Nazareth surely lies in his elusiveness. Even in Christian scripture he is presented variously by different authors. St Paul, our first witness to his existence, barely mentions him as a human being at all, other than to focus on his death and resurrection and the alleged meaning for us of his exaltation as Christ. The three "synoptic" gospels, the gospel of John and the Book of Revelation portray Jesus in strikingly contrasting ways, as do non-Biblical early Christian texts.

In my lifetime another ancient writing, the Gospel of Thomas, lost for millennia, has presented a further, compelling antique face of Jesus, that of riddling mage. There have been hundreds of so-called "true stories" of Jesus published, each containing "information" supposedly suppressed by the Church and now "at last" revealed. Jesus has been pictured as charismatic healer, freedom fighter, purveyor of management wisdom, guarantor of empires, wandering holy man, libertine, founder of dynasties, Californian cool dude and really, whatever authors, nations, churches have needed him to be.

He may perhaps inhabit some or all of those roles. It might be in the job-description of Christ to shape-shift, to come to each of us in a way we can receive and understand.

How Jesus Christ first came to me was, as described above, in the underwhelming guise of pale unleavened bread: Christ's silent presence seemed the more powerful for the bread's very plainness and lack of glamour.

Jesus is presented in the gospels and in classic Christian literature as on the one hand fully human (albeit virginally conceived). On the other, he is a "face" of the mysterious divine, entering our human history and bloodstream. "In the beginning" says St John "was the Word, and the Word was with God, and the Word was God." (John 1:1)

That "Word" (or Logos) had been concealed all along in what gives coherence, order and beauty to the stuff of creation; but now the "God who is strictly un-speakable by finite beings...speaks himself in and as an entirely finite subject, wholly flesh and blood, mortal and vulnerable."[21] Another far subtler version of "God said" channelled through vagaries of culture and custom and language and tradition.

But what this "face" of the divine went on to say, or rather, cry, alarmingly, was "My God, my God why have you forsaken me?" (Matthew 27:46) That has been the howl of creation from the big bang till now.

Much reflection on Jesus, both in the New Testament and since, focuses on the failure of his immediate mission and the infliction on him of humiliation, terror, desolation and death. There's no reason necessarily to presume the human Jesus expected any of that.

When the story of Jesus' betrayal, abandonment and

---

21 Rowan Williams, Christ the Heart of Creation, Bloomsbury Continuum, 2018, p.234

crucifixion is re-enacted, which it is every year during what we still call Holy Week, it never fails to grip some people by its pathos, wrong-headedness and tragedy.

We cannot, of course, ultimately know what did or didn't happen, then or at any other time in the past; we might say only God can know such stuff. What Christians claim with certainty is that the drama of Christ's "passion" has had a cathartic effect down the centuries...mostly for the good, though not always. It expresses something later Jewish sages called "the breaking of the vessels"[22]: chaos as a necessary, tragic dimension of life. We all know freedom is freedom for things to go, from our human perspective, horribly wrong. That doesn't need spelling out, for you or me.

Thus we can see the Jesus story as a magnificent improvisation in our earthly snake-pit. Even reading the considered lines of the official Gospels, you can observe the man's human awareness evolving[23]. Actions didn't necessarily have desired consequences: and the unfolding disaster of his betrayal and arrest partook of a factor in our make-up impossible to predict or ignore, the "crack in everything" memorably described by songwriter Leonard Cohen.[24]

What followed, and what of course makes the story so compelling, is what Jesus did with this disaster, how he improvised round it to turn it into a sacrament of forgiveness and healing and liberation. So that the sign of the cross, symbol of oppression and horror, became an icon of hope, a window onto grace: something we wear round

---

22 (In the Kabbalah as taught by Isaac Luria and his disciples).

23 See for instance Matthew 15:22–28

24 In Anthem, 1992. "Forget your perfect offering/ There is a crack in everything/ That's how the light gets in."

our necks, use to console widows and cling to when all else disintegrates.

I have had a very fortunate life. I've been dragged (kicking and resisting) into the service of one meandering current in the river of religious practice that flows from Jesus Christ. Part of that service, over many years, has been the privilege of presiding at the Eucharist, Mass, Holy Communion, Lord's Supper...several names are used.

There may, for all I know, have been a "Sacred Contract"[25] entered into shortly before I came into this world, suggesting lineaments of a life, what experiences I might enjoy, what gifts I might offer. Maybe that triggered my infant sense of homecoming when at Mass.

However, details of my journey, as of yours, are improvised: made up as we go along. We pick up and run with what happens to be lying around; and what's lying around at any moment is a result of haphazard events, decisions recent and distant, accidents of battle and genetics, random baggage.

In short: our lives are not scripted, by God or anyone else.

But nor are they completely and utterly random. There are parameters, archetypes, itineraries. It has often seemed to me help is available, visible and invisible, if we care to call on it.

Meanwhile, the improvisation goes on. It never comes to an end: which is why "Stay awake" is so frequently what we're told, in the gospels and elsewhere.

So on the night before he died, Jesus took the probable course of events, melded them with already-ancient

25 Carolyn Myss, Sacred Contacts, Three Rivers, 2002, p.3 and ff.

human reflexes of sacrifice and offering, and invented a new-old ceremony in which his abyss might be activated as a universal prayer of hope: "do this in remembrance of me" (Luke 22:19). (The "crack in everything" has of course meant that Jesus' sign of healing and reconciliation has itself been used to divide and exclude).

When the ceremony, whether it's called Mass or Holy Communion or Eucharist or the Lord's Supper or whatever, takes place, what we believe we're doing is entering into a moment both within and outside time, in which a great "Amen" is sounded. "Amen" is an ancient cry of recognition: it reaffirms friendship between our present here and now and the ultimate vibration we might call God, Father or Mother, Brahman, Allah, origin, source, silence, emptiness... "Amen" is brother to the Aramaic word Jesus might have used when he said "Your faith has saved you"(e.g. Mark 5:34) It's also sister to "Om", sound of the essence of reality in Indian religions. Amen celebrates connection: not being completely random in an uncaring cosmos. You choose to say Amen, Om. You can choose not to say it. For a while, I chose not to do so.

At Holy Communion, Jesus Christ's judicial murder is presented, not as another sordid crime in humanity's long list but as a sign of "The Love that moves the sun and the other stars". "Who made there by his one oblation of himself once offered" wrote Thomas Cranmer many years later[26], "a full, perfect and sufficient sacrifice, oblation and satisfaction, for the sins of the whole world." Those magisterial words articulate a shared understanding of Jesus' action as not merely human but divine.

That was what he improvised his death into. We re-enact Jesus' so-called Last Supper to remind ourselves of

---

26 In the Eucharistic Prayer of the Book of Common Prayer.

a mystical feast or rainbow connecting earth and heaven, formed from his body represented by bread and his blood represented by wine. Every enactment of Holy Communion, in my tradition at any rate, is called a Celebration, even if it takes place at a funeral or on a battlefield or in some reeking hellhole of fear. What's being celebrated is connection: openness to presence, openness to wonder.

But of course none of that would be known by any of us, were it not for what is alleged to have happened after Jesus' death. What are we to make of the resurrection stories in the four authorised gospels? They have been meditated on for two millennia. Each story is a doorway into mystery; in each, some especial facet sparkles. (The love of Mary Magdalene is one ingredient which has always fascinated me, along with many of my generation).

And yet our earliest witness to Christ, St Paul, based his whole fiery ministry, not on any of the memories written down by the gospel-writers, but on an encounter he believed himself to have had with the risen Christ. And that's surely how it was for the first generation of Jesus-followers and how it has been ever since: what is called Easter faith often has to do with a perceived nearness to the human sphere of Jesus Christ, a sense that people have of him being in some unexplained way a friend here and now, not some distant historical figure. When people in the West first experience love of God, it may often be love for Jesus they actually encounter. Jesus can inhabit this or that role, and turn people's lives around, seemingly as a living being. That's what people mean when they talk about the risen Christ.

Hence, from very early on, they called Jesus "Lord". That was not just any designation. Yes, it was the highest and mightiest title people could come up with at that time.

But it was also what had been used by Greek-speakers

to indicate the placing in Jewish scripture of four Hebrew letters, YHWH. That formula is an inner, mystical "name" supposed never to be pronounced or spoken. Its appearances were screened, in the Bible used by some of Jesus' earliest followers, by the word "Lord."

Thus, when they said "Lord" about Jesus, they were connecting their crucified and risen teacher with the One who had spoken to Moses out of the burning bush, who had guided and chastised Israel and who was worshipped at Jerusalem and amongst the rabbis.

Jesus of Nazareth, Palestinian Roman-era carpenter and healer, executed as a felon, was thus acclaimed as nothing less than a transmission of the Most High, of YHWH. And that's more or less how people in Christian parts of our little planet have continued to see Jesus ("God-With-Us") and why they love him...while historically taking scant notice of the core of his reported message, about compassionate conversion of life.

No-one can say finally and definitively what YHWH means, though many claim to. "I Am" is a popular interpretation, and certainly has the virtue of clarity. More on "I Am" in a moment, but undoubtedly YHWH is indicative of presence, and continues to represent awesome living mystery to millions of Jewish people and to many others.

There are of course numerous "names" given to God. Even in the Bible there are many, though YHWH is considered by Jewish people to come first. Other revered and beloved streams of spiritual practice each have their cherished "names"...Allah and Brahman being obvious examples, but as you well know there are as many others as there are grains of sand on the seashore.

Each, if we had time, would be worth careful scrutiny. Each may witness to presence in some uniquely important way or other. Each might have something special to disclose.

And each is a joke between a limited group of humans and the boundless luminosity by which they believe themselves to have been befriended.

Similarly, powerful hope-inducing presence is what many contemporaries of mine continue to discover in the name of Jesus Christ: truly, a friend in high places, seemingly able to take on localised guises and intervene unpredictably and for the good in the lives of individuals. "How sweet the name of Jesus sounds in a believer's ear!" wrote the converted slave-captain John Newton in 1779. He spoke, to put it mildly, for many.

Jesus' sufferings, too, mark him out as one who knows what it is to be human, to be wounded, to feel forsaken... to die. "O God, make speed to save us; O Lord, make haste to help us."[27]

Nevertheless, my own connection with this wonder-worker has often not been as literal or vivid as others have described. I've been, at times, a somewhat distant disciple, lingering on the edge of the tent, then wandering off.

I have been impressed, of course, by some (not all) of what emanates from Jesus Christ. I have no difficulty believing he shows us a face of absolute *being*, that he makes the unknown knowable. Here is one way:

In John's gospel, there are seven riddles by Christ each beginning with the words "I am": "I am the bread of life" (John 6:35), "I am the light of the world" (8:12), "I am the door" (10:9), "I am the good shepherd (10:11,14), "I am the

---

27 Opening versicle and response at Matins and Evensong in the Book of Common Prayer, based on Psalm 70:1

resurrection and the life" (11:25), "I am the way, the truth and the life" (14:6), "I am the vine" (15: 1,5).

There is no-one on earth potentially unable to say, or think, "I am." It's a gift we are all given. And, as mentioned earlier, "I Am" is a purported "name" of God.

"I am" is the great attribute shared indiscriminately by all. When Jesus says "I am" he is not indicating something uniquely true of him: here is the teacher who invites his students to "follow him" and become as he is.

By using that everyday phrase and consecrating what we all share, namely *being*, Jesus Christ in John's gospel transcends time, place and scriptural significance and draws close alongside my life and yours at this moment. For "I am", right here, right now. "I am" wrote these words. "I am" is reading them. You can say "I am" in your depths, I in mine. We know we *are*.

And then "I Am", *being*, is gently revealed: as presence. Immanuel. God-With-Us.

And yet I have still wandered off.

To me Jesus Christ has been somewhat like an (irritatingly wonderful) older cousin, whose experience and wisdom are formative, though I've sometimes felt a need to ignore him or do the opposite. He has not been my only guru, and one of the many excellent things about cousin Jesus is: in no way does he insist on being so. On the contrary, he appears to rejoice in a vast company of friends of whom he is, as it were, first among equals.

He pays no attention to "nothing-but", or to transient "normality", or to what "everyone thinks" (least of all to what Christians think).

It's an improvisation, this life you and I are in. It's often been compared to some kind of dance, with or without dance-steps, which we continue to learn (or not) as we go on.

The presence I've spoken of is not now, for me, focussed in Eucharistic bread. Long ago I discovered one can just as well be open to Christ in one's own being, in a landscape or the blue sky above or in another person's eyes...

We've been given another "I am" in my lifetime, through the Gospel of Thomas, mentioned earlier: "I am the light that is over all things. I am all: from me all came forth, and to me all attained. Split a piece of wood; I am there. Lift up the stone, and you will find me there." (Gospel of Thomas, 77). The very cosmos, the whole ludicrous beautiful terrifying dance, as an ongoing evolving sacrament: that's what cousin Jesus casually showed us, while sashaying by.

No reason to suppose any of that will resonate with you. But I hope something does, and unbolts the trap door in your heart.

There is another factor. Cousin Jesus had his own intimate name for God, and that was Abba. It speaks of a connection, an umbilical cord: that this "God" is not just "another thing" but part of us, part of "I am" in a way comparable to our earthly father or mother.

And a habit Jesus demonstrated was going off into the wilderness to commune with Abba (see for instance Mark 1:35). Sharing as he did in human life, some of what Jesus communicated might have been fierce and agonized, and we're told that near the end of his dying there came a terrible cry, "My God, my God, why have you forsaken me?" Christ's meditation was not all necessarily serene and blissful.

And that gives a clue about our own potentialities.

SIX

In the "Great Plague" that struck London in 1665, "It was reported that the living, out of despair, sometimes flung themselves among the dead...and when, at night, the drunken heard the rumble of the dead cart and the noise of the iron bell they came to the window and jeered at anyone who mourned for the newly dead. They also uttered 'blasphemous expressions' such as 'There is no God' or 'God is a devil'."[28] Comparable acts have taken place at all times; and suchlike events will be going on now. Terror, grief and loss are inescapable. There may be a strong urge to blasphemy or despair.

But there is also, among us humans, an instinct to pray. On behalf of people who can't protect themselves, who are perhaps brutalised or sick or dying. For whom "it's all fuckin' shit."

We humans are occasionally valiant, creative and beautiful. Sometimes we are scumbags. We all die, irrespective.

In oneness with vulnerable, suffering humans, beautiful and scumbag alike, at this moment and maybe every moment, there's an instinct to cry out: "My God, my God, why have you forsaken us?"

I can't guess the answer. But to make that prayer, alongside the broken wounded Christ, seems to me one valid response to the terror and sadness of life... the "brokenness of the vessels." It's not denying the love of God to do that. The Psalms of ancient Israel are full of such remonstrations (Jesus' cry is of course the opening line of Psalm 22). It becomes possible fully and truly to confess and express your inner being, heart, soul, guts, and all, when your "I am" is in true alignment with the great "I Am", however that might be imagined.

---

28 Peter Ackroyd, London, The Biography, Vintage, 2001, p.204

Such alignment is triggered in the first place through love. Through *noticing* what I have called presence (just a word, provisional as any other), through giving attention to presence wherever we first become aware of it.

That might be in stories or words of Jesus, or other scripture. It might be in sacrament, as for me when a child, or in silence, as often now. Or in the warmth and noise of a kitchen. Or the voices of swallows screaming overhead, or... the surge of the tide, or... the stupendousness of the night sky, or... the juddering roar of a motorcycle, or...

...it matters not: "God is everywhere". Say "I am": listen to your heart. Let your heart awaken (and your whole body) so you can recognise your love-link with I Am, the heart of all.

SEVEN

Seeing that he answered them well, he asked

It's 1968. I am with a tall, long-haired hippyish man laughing and giggling in a garden in lovely autumn sunshine with two girls in short flimsy dresses; one of the girls is wearing a straw hat. We are only a few miles down the busy road from my Catholic church and school. But it seems I've arrived in another country.

Though a teacher, the man likes to be known by his first name, Jonathan. He wears a greatcoat, beads and John Lennon glasses and affects an air of tolerant superiority. Someone has told me he's a "pothead", but I've no idea what that means. Jonathan has just informed us he's "spiritual but not religious." It's the first time I have heard that phrase.

Like thousands of other privileged but failed adolescents in England at that time, I had become an art student. I was sixteen. I had a portfolio of tortured teenage paintings in expressionist mode to present at what passed for an interview. Grants were easy to come by.

A condition of a grant, however, was that one did some general studies along with the art. Colleges could decide what such studies might consist of.

Jonathan claims to be a student of Freudian psychology. So he has been given the task of informing us sixteen year olds about our egos and super egos.

It turns out, however, he is chiefly interested in the id. Sex, he says, is not only the main ingredient of happiness: it's what we're made for, what the point of life is. He casts a superior eye round the female students. They sit with heads bowed, silently doodling in their notepads.

Another lesson on my new timetable is Life Drawing. This will involve a naked model, possibly female. Pretending to look forward to it, I actually feel fear at the prospect of seeing a real grown-up woman naked. Hard to believe now, but at sixteen I have never yet seen one in real life.

However, when the model steps out from behind a curtain, she is so scrawny she might be a teenage boy. Her arms have many red blotches, and she also has bruises in various places. Over coffee in between poses, as she gets to know us, sitting in her flimsy dressing-gown, she tells us the melancholy story of her life, her addictions, pregnancies, violent partners. As I listen to her, I begin to understand a little the point of some of the Catholic prohibitions around sex. And yet she seems a gutsy, intelligent, curious person, vulnerable but also full of love. Her name is Georgie.

In one of the stories about Jesus I often heard read as a child, he was eating at the house of a religious leader. A woman had come in while they were eating, and was weeping and massaging Jesus' feet with oil and wiping them with her hair. The host was scandalised, but Jesus' response to him began with the words, "Do you see this woman? (Luke 7:44)

Thinking now about Georgie, it seems extraordinary to remember how she opened up to us, a random assortment of teenage girls and boys. And we really liked her, and laughed at some of her tales; and she seemed to like us. It was as though we "saw" her, in a way deeper than any of us had expected, and she "saw" us...and something magical passed between us.

SEVEN

I have never forgotten her.

The tutor of our Life Drawing class, a lively snappily-suited man called Mr Morgan, talked as Georgie posed, exhorting us to notice not only the exact way she was positioned, but the fall of light from the high windows across her limbs and across the room. "This moment" he enthused "has never been before in the history of the world. And we will never be in this moment ever again. Look! Really look! Imagine you've been blind all your life, and suddenly you can see. Look at it all! Notice the pose! Pay attention to this moment: it will never be repeated!"

He would go on and on like this, leaping round Georgie waving his arms about. He was trying to get us to observe properly so we could draw. But it seemed to me, even at the time, a thrilling invitation to wake up; and I've often found myself repeating his words in my head as I inhabit another new day.

Attention! That's one vital key, not just to Life Drawing but to life. "Don't think about the future" famously wrote Ram Dass a few years later, "just be HERE NOW. Don't think about the past. Just be HERE NOW."[29] A thrilling, vital reminder, though obviously we can't actually shut ourselves off from past and future. But the present is just that, present. "If not now," says Eckhart Tolle, "when?"[30]

I had been exhorted endlessly, drearily, in my former life, about the importance of faith. And now here was someone with no explicit religious faith, opening a door by exhorting us to pay attention to the present moment: and instantly energy, fresh air, came blasting in.

Not that the art college was without openly-stated

---

29 Ram Dass, Be Here Now, Lama Foundation, 1971, p.90
30 Eckhart Tolle, The Power of Now, Hodder and Stoughton, 1999, p.43

philosophical principles. Those were made clear in the mandatory general studies lectures, which set out a view of life explicitly nihilist.

It followed that though the social mores of the college were let-it-all-hang-out liberal (with a strong presumption of male chauvinism), the artistic credo was very definitely puritan...and this was "True Faith", not negotiable. Representation, content, meaning, purpose and suchlike obsolete notions were all to be eliminated, and "... artists were finally left with only the self-reflective and fairly paralyzing preoccupation with their own creative processes..."[31]

Jonathan, our "spiritual but not religious" tutor, enacted this to perfection. He used to sit for hours in front of huge white canvases. He would perch there meditatively, stroking his chin. Eventually, he would saunter up and make a few splodges in the top left-hand corner. He would then declare the work complete. Other staff members seemed to take this seriously and consider him an advanced practitioner.

"Man knows at last" wrote Jacques Monod in 1970, "that he is alone in the indifferent immensity of the universe, whence he has emerged by chance. His duty, like his fate, is written nowhere."[32] That bracing pronouncement, much-quoted at the time, remains a forceful expression of heroic nihilism.

Such nihilism must be faced into, by anyone claiming to be on a spiritual quest. The "indifferent immensity of the universe" is what we all encounter, daily.

---

31 Richard Tarnas, The Passion of the Western Mind, Pimlico, 1991, p.392

32 Jacques Monod, trans. A.Wainhouse, Chance and Necessity, Fontana, 1971, p.171

SEVEN

The immediate effect of such nihilism on us art students, however, was "...an end point in which all that remained was a blank canvas..."[33]

General anathemas against form and meaning were widely fashionable at the time. However, seemingly by chance I met a man called Osmund Caine. He was a dissenting Catholic, ran a highly-regarded graphic design course, and when the time came to graduate to more advanced studies, he was willing to accept me as a student.

Mr Caine was not, to put it mildly, in thrall to the zeitgeist. A mighty figure, tall, grey-bearded, he looked every inch a patriarch from some past age. Artistically a disciple of the painter Stanley Spencer, Mr Caine was far beyond the horizon of aesthetic trendiness, about which he cared not a jot. His paintings and stained glass windows were traditionally crafted and superbly executed. They continue to adorn public and private spaces, and to communicate with people...considerably more than can be said for Jonathan's blobs.

Osmund Caine was also a man of esoteric spiritual fervour. Sometimes this would expose him to mockery, behind his back (no-one would have dared ridicule him to his face). Classes supposedly about illustration technique might veer off into lengthy monologues on the astrology of stone circles or the deeper meanings of Arthurian legends. Many of my fellow students found this laughable.

I'm ashamed to say I went along with some of the laughter. Humans are pack animals, unfortunately. And we students were know-it-all nineteen-year-olds.

But a door into the so-called Western Mystery tradition, of which he was a devotee, was left ajar by this gruff,

33 Richard Tarnas, ibid, p.393

august man. And, while pretending to laugh with the others, I accepted, timidly, Mr Caine's invitation. I went, secretly, and drew (and when no-one was looking, hugged) the mighty standing stones at Avebury. I crept away and spent some nights alone on Glastonbury Tor. I didn't know what I was expecting to find there. But what I witnessed, unforgettably, was the magic of dawn across the Somerset levels.

Mr Caine encouraged us to go out and draw from nature, at that time an unfashionable activity. One day, I sat on a muddy bank of the Thames, sketching some trees on the other side. Suddenly, it was as though, while remaining in the present moment, I had become tuned to an unexpected frequency, in which trees communicate. One tree in particular seemed to have noticed me noticing it, and was throwing a beam of love across the churning river straight into my heart. There were other people on the opposite bank, and they were unconcerned, just behaving as normal. But I was transfixed, couldn't leave the spot. I just wanted to sit there and look and look, to commune with this tree that was in love with me and I with it... I realise how ridiculous that will seem, unless you've encountered something similar in the presence of nature, and then it won't seem ridiculous at all.

Thousands of people enjoy such experiences. I have, numerous times since. But that was the first. And it came completely out of the blue. I had no idea such things happened, nor any language in which to express it. Later, I would discover mysterious portals do appear and disappear in nature. Through them we humans sometimes glimpse, to our surprise, interiority, connectedness, presence. The universe in its immensity can seem far from indifferent at such moments.

For the mandatory general studies ingredient of his design course, Mr Caine had hired someone as unusual as himself: a young, softly spoken scholar of esoteric wisdom. Mr Caine's employment of this man was a powerful two-finger to supposed normality. The tutor was gentle and smiling, and he attempted with humorous patience to open our reluctant minds to some of the knowledge of past ages.

One of the beginners' courses this teacher ran was on the Jewish mystical system known as Kabbalah, or the Tree of Life. Kabbalah offers a sophisticated map of presence, how earth and heaven supposedly mesh. I was instantly enthralled, and did turgid teenage paintings on Kabbalistic themes to prove it.

But I was too timid, too much wanting acceptance by my teenaged cohort, to express any of that enthusiasm at the time. Initiation requires some community of like-minded people in whose company one can learn and share experiences. Nothing was available to me, or so it seemed...certainly the Church I'd walked away from was the last place I would have considered sharing spiritual experiences or enthusiasms.

And yet it is through apparently chance encounters with individuals that we are helped on our way in any quest for wisdom or enlightenment. I don't pretend to know how this works, how the levers are pulled in heaven, as it were. All I know is, it does work. There is randomness involved. But within that randomness, improvisations happen, connections occur, patterns emerge... then they vanish again, and the dance goes on.

You may have heard an old saying, "when the student is ready the teacher appears." Your external way-shower might be a swami in a remote retreat. But just as likely it might be someone you meet at a bus stop. There is an ancient Christian doctrine called the "Communion of

Saints" that is partly about how we, vulnerable ignorant humans, give and receive encouragement to one another along the way. Georgie and Mr Morgan might be startled indeed to learn they were temporary saints, bearers of divine grace and encouragement to me: but they most definitely were.

And so was a man I never properly thanked at the time (because I was uncomprehending and a bit afraid of him): Osmund Caine, artist and teacher. He demonstrated, when everything seemed covered in concrete, that certain of the older pathways might still be located, and that they remain open and life-giving. To his example, and to his generosity of spirit, I owe much.

But the big world of "normality" was hostile to mystical adventures. It remains so.

EIGHT

The Lord our God (ii)

According to the Kabbalah I began to learn about all those years ago, when the worlds were created, the Holy One contracted ("Tzimtzum" in Hebrew) so that there could be a void where God is not. Such a void "...is the place of origin of freedom...which is absolute potentiality, not in any way determined. And all of the beings...carry within themselves a 'drop' of the void and a 'spark' of God."[34]

Tzimtzum, contested though it is, feels to me a compelling myth of the life we often experience: "God-forsaken", yet yearning for home. Jesus Christ's cry from the cross "My God, my God, why have you forsaken me?" powerfully expresses Tzimtzum both in its horror and its wonder.

According to some at least of its Jewish proponents, Tzimtzum is actually no more than concealment. "Do I not fill the heaven and the earth?" (Jeremiah 23:24). "It is the 'hiding of God' that allows us to perceive ourselves as separate...But...there has never been any separation...God is here, now, in this very space."[35]

Yet the seeming absence of God might be almost as vital to our human flourishing as any glimmer of heaven. God's apparent absence might be a paradoxical ground of our

---

34 Meditations on the Tarot, p.85
35 Zalman Schachter-Shalomi and Netanel Miles-Yepes: God Hidden, Whereabouts Unknown. Albion, 2013, p.28

freedom. Atheism might be necessary, not only for us to do proper science but to get on with our everyday lives. We need not marvel at that. But nor need we be compelled to accept secular ideologies of "nothing-but." A most important part of our graduation from zygotes to full human stature is simple longing.

Maybe exile from home is what enables us to grow. But in order for that to happen, there does needs to be a rumour of home's reality... some connection however faint...the "daughter of a voice"...

Throughout human history, the rumour has sometimes seemed to vanish. It had vanished for the old man with his pramload of junk who I witnessed plodding along when I was a child. There will be no shortage of people, wherever or whenever you are reading this, whose circumstances are hellish. What would be the point, for them, of offering banalities about "God's love?" Or, what light could possibly dawn on those whose whole being has become wrapped in murderous evil?

I don't know. The brilliant and compassionate young Jewish Dutchwoman Etty Hillesum wrote of guards at Westerbork concentration camp in 1943, "When I think of the faces of that squad of armed, green-uniformed guards-my God, those faces! I looked at them, each in turn, from behind the safety of a window, and I have never been so frightened of anything in my life. I sank to my knees with the words that preside over human life: And God made man after His likeness. That passage spent a difficult morning with me."[36]

"God is everywhere." In the actions of those SS guards and others like them? In the plague bacillus? Under the

---

36 Etty Hillesum, trans. Arnold J.Pomerans: An Interrupted Life: Diaries and Letters 1941–43, Persephone 1999, p.402

rubble of buildings brought down in earthquakes or inundated by tsunamis? In our cat as she torments a fieldmouse?

Such questions are of course also banalities, but they were not lost on me at the time.

I emerged from the warm but cloying embrace of my religious childhood and the romantic mysticism encouraged by Osmund Caine, and began work in London as a designer. As I climbed the escalator at Holborn station for my first morning at work, "alone in the indifferent immensity of the universe" might not be a bad description of how I felt.

One of the really uncomfortable challenges facing any young adult is surely the whole matter of fashioning a persona: who we are, in our own eyes and in the eyes of others (made even more daunting by electronic media). The world into which I was launched was completely consumerist; and though it was necessary casually to demonstrate atheism in order to be part of the tribe, there were in fact whole pantheons of secular gods competing for worship.

So who am I, through the lens of this unimaginably powerful industrial capitalist consumerist religion which perpetually strives to occupy and enslave the imaginations of us all?

Forget "I am." I am nobody, other than what I achieve or possess or am possessed by.

So, like most of the males around me, I set about fashioning a persona while consuming quantities of alcohol and exploring the turgid streets of the city in pursuit of something alleged to be love. (Part of me recognised that as a culturally-generated compulsion. But the god demanded sacrifice).

In Kabbalah, the Tree of Life is a picture of how divine energies participate in creation. At the centre of the Tree is a highway represented from Tiphareth, the human heart, through the Void of unknowing to Kether, so-called "Crown" of creation and "En Soph," infinite Other. So far, so straightforward?

But there are side-branches bearing fruit; and they too are divine energies. To the middle left, for instance, we find Geburah, "Severity." That has to do with boundaries. But Geburah can easily become, not servant but master, not fruit of the divine but god in its own right. Those young prison guards Etty Hillesum spoke of had become devotees of this imposter, trapped in their murderous worship of cleansing and exclusion and retribution.

And at the Tree's lower right is a branch, Netzach, bearing fruits of instinct and creativity and sex, glorious burgeoning energies of adulthood. But that, throughout my life, has been mistaken for the central power and adored as god in its own right.

It was Netzach, or some very warped, distorted and diminished version of it, that I spent too many weary hours hunting down, chasing pavements to little or no avail.

"Freud" wrote Carl Jung "never asked himself why he was compelled to talk continually of sex, why the idea had taken such possession of him. He remained unaware that his 'monotony of interpretation' expressed flight from... that other side of him which might perhaps be called mystical..."[37] Jonathan, my "spiritual but not religious" art school tutor, had gone on and on about the Freudian id as though it were the key that would unlock all of life's mysteries.

---

37 C.J.Jung, Memories, Dreams, Reflections, Flamingo 1983, p.175

But deep within us, represented at the centre of the Tree of Life by Tiphareth, is the need not just for horizontal connections, but for experiences of truth: for that "connection with the higher powers" William James referred to. "Around this need everything else...is arranged like planets round the sun."[38]

My attempts to fashion a persona, my compulsive pavement-chasing, were about as creative as Jonathan's long sessions in front of empty canvases. "The Tao reduced to the id" Ken Wilber wrote contemptuously, many years later.[39]

I didn't understand any of that at the time. By 1974 I was working for a national newspaper in the centre of London. On a form circulated round employees that year was a question about religion. I proudly wrote NONE in the box. This was how I was trying to fashion my persona: not some crank.

In John's gospel, when Jesus has been arrested, Simon Peter is warming himself by a brazier outside the High Priest's house. A servant asks, is he not one of the man's disciples (John 18:25) and Peter answers "I am" and then adds the little word "not."

---

38 Jacob Needleman, Lost Christianity, Element 1990, p.61
39 Ken Wilber, Sex, Ecology, Spirituality, Shambala 2000, p. 500

NINE

...is one

Here am I, walking up Fleet Street, still at that time the epicentre of the British news media, one afternoon in the mid-1970s. Before me Ludgate Circus, bisected in those days by a railway bridge, and the familiar dome and front of St Paul's, beside me the perpetual grind of traffic, all around me men and women purposefully hurrying. Warm energy vibrating from offices and from pubs where much business is being done and vast quantities of liquor put away. Rumours. Rumours flowing up and down the street... you can almost see them, a swarm, a murmuration, never ceasing. Young men run from one office or pub to another, "Have you heard?"

Our office was off the main Street, amid the lanes and alleyways between St Paul's and the river. It was an indescribably noisy, smoky, agitated place, typewriters clacking, phones ringing non-stop, people shouting at one another, occasional politicians or sports celebrities wandering through. Sometimes the whole building shook as the presses thundered. How I loved it! How I love the memory of it!

As a respite from the noise, I would sometimes wander the old lanes and alleyways. There were still Blitz bomb-craters in a few places, covered in wild flowers. Sitting in the tiny burial ground of a church destroyed in the 1666 Great Fire, surrounded by the clattering of typewriters from Victorian offices, it was easy to get a sense of tumultuous tides of human life that had raged through that place in times past. I used to begin to imagine I was communing with souls of people who had lived there long ago, and then stop myself: ridiculous behaviour for an atheist.

Other days I used to go and sit in St Paul's... also unorthodox behaviour. Once when I was sitting there, a young clergyman came and sat with me. He was African, and it soon became apparent he was extremely homesick and unhappy. He told me how he had come to England expecting to find a land of faith, and was amazed by the indifference and materialism all around him. He felt he had been lied to by those who had sent him here. I noticed he was in tears, and I put an arm round him to comfort him. I said that I was unable to share his faith, but that I wished him well. He seemed an impressive young man, if naive: there was something beautiful about him, strong, noble, sincere. Did I really think his faith wrong-headed?

When I got back to the office, I mentioned the conversation to one of my managers, a hard-drinking laddish man in pinstripe suit and braces. He replied, "Don't be bloody stupid, you're no bloody atheist, you're a Christian humanist. That's just what you are. Get over it, you arsehole." He then added, "I hate bloody Christians...the humanist bit I can just about cope with."

That Christmas Eve I went to stay overnight with my parents and out of politeness went to Midnight Mass at the church where I had once served. As Mass went on I hated being there. The altar boys were incompetent, whispering and giggling among themselves. The old priest stumbled through ritual and words, clumsy, inebriated, absent. I felt contempt. Never again! What a load of nonsense...

...and suddenly it was as though a gentle, amiable bolt of lightning touched the crown of my head and passed down my spine to my feet, making the whole body tingle, and with it a message, not in words but clear, explicit, "It's OK to think this is nonsense. But it isn't. And you are wanted."

An extraordinary moment, and gone as soon as it was come.

But I did not consider myself a "believer" in any sense of the word. I couldn't imagine an understanding of faith higher, wider or deeper than the childhood one I had rejected. "Dead to life, dead to the body, dead to sex, dead to beauty, dead to excellence: that never was a real God anyway..."[40] Ken Wilber was not to write those words for another thirty years, but they express what I felt, passionately, about the God of the "True Faith" back in 1974.

In Trinitarian Christian imagery, there is a third "face" of the divine beside the transcendent "Abba" and Jesus Christ the "Son." This third "face" is called the Holy Spirit, and is sometimes pictured as a dove (Mark 1.10). That image expresses purity, love and connection (doves are supposed to be faithful, gregarious birds).

But the Holy Spirit is also oneness of being flowing between what we call unknowable and the realm of the known: connectedness, form, meaning. Differentiated...yet one. Love flowing continuously between them.

Such is the "wisdom" Jesus famously likened to a wind, that "blows where it chooses, and you hear the sound of it, but you do not know where it comes from, or where it goes..." (John 3:8)

"The Holy Spirit is...": any sentence beginning with those words is likely to be nonsense. But it will be beautiful nonsense, about inspiration. Musicians, actors, surgeons,

---

40 Ken Wilber, Integral Spirituality, Integral Books, 2007, p.206

scientists in their laboratories, writers, artists, sportspeople: however skilful, all may experience something that leads them out beyond themselves. The Holy Spirit is imagined as the divine "face" behind that. She is sometimes personified in scripture as a graceful woman, or imagined as divine breath (e.g. the exquisite lines in Wisdom 7:22ff), or pictured as fire (Acts 2:3).

She is seen as both empowering traditions and necessarily breaking them. In many of our stories of Spirit there is a quality of playfulness. Scriptures are claimed to be "Spirit-breathed."

The Holy Spirit is also imagined sparking reactions and collisions between unexpected people. The African priest and my erstwhile manager are two who, for me, seemed to act as momentary conduits of her scarifying grace. We might be privileged occasionally to act in this way for one another (rather than as censorious sneer-vipers, into which we are ever prone to shrivel).

But then again, the Holy Spirit is described as working through our quiet minds when we enter into stillness. In his letter to the Romans, St Paul mentions a strange phenomenon whereby it sometimes feels as though we are not so much praying ourselves as being prayed through: "... that very Spirit intercedes with sighs too deep for words." (Romans 8:26)

In such images, we humans have attempted the impossible: to describe the wellspring of being. Jesus himself did it with his icon of an attentive Father with whom we might communicate secretly: "...go into your room and shut the door and pray to your Father who is in secret..." (Matthew 6:6). That was the story I was told as a child: the invisible Father watching over us. I had put it away, along with other "childish things."

The traditional stories have their time and place. They radiate light. But we load them with too much freight when we claim they give diagrammatic certainty: how could they? The crack that runs through everything runs through them too: hence the appalling cry to his Abba of Christ from the cross: "My God, my God, why have you forsaken me?" (Matthew 27: 46). That is the cry of nature down the ages. It's frequently "all fuckin' shit", at ground level.

I knew that. I also knew that at root I disbelieved the atheism we were supposed to espouse, didn't like what it did to me, considered it just as cracked as any religious certainty. For better or worse, my reflexes were Christian, as the manager had observed (not "good", merely Christian). Near where I worked, the "lost" River Fleet, built over and forgotten, was still roaring to the Thames in dark underground gullies. Pretending it was not there had not made it go away.

About that time, I met a woman who was in the habit of sometimes going to church, which had helped her through a lonely childhood. She suggested we might go together. I resisted. But eventually I said yes.

The church was Anglican. I had sometimes listened to choral Anglican services in cathedrals and suchlike places. The people at this church took no notice of me, which was fine. No one asked what I was doing there.

It was an interesting historic building. One day I decided to go and have a look, read the monuments, enjoy the architecture. There was a bookstall at the back, and in it I found something by a man called Thomas Corbishley, a Jesuit priest, in which I read the following words: "...if ever a man or woman ought to be absolutely and uninhibitedly personal it is surely in the expression of a relationship which...is unique and unrepeated in the whole of the universe."[41]

"Right," I thought a little later, alone at home with the blinds drawn, "this is real. No pretence. I really, for once and for all, want to know. If you are there, please show me."

And heaven opened, or at any rate the tiny grain of heaven accessible to me.

One is supposed not to talk about "religious experience" because in so doing one falsifies and travesties it. However, this happened over forty years ago as I am writing now, and it was the most significant of my various epiphanies in that it was something which, once experienced, could not be denied or gone back from.

How it felt was as if the whole of my inside, from the heart, had suddenly shifted, as if there was a previously unknown sluice gate that had opened and floodwaters of light and joy were welling up.

It's difficult to describe because it's not really comparable to anything in the everyday world at all...

...it was felt rather than seen...

...as though suddenly I was swimming in limitless light, a creature of sunlit depths, basking in bliss.

It went on for, I don't know how long, it felt a long time.

Eventually, I wanted to put my feet back on the ground, and said "thank you, please can it stop?" And gently, the sluice gate closed, the waters receded, and I was back in my room with blinds drawn, able to hear people and traffic and normality.

But I discovered I could re-enter the experience pretty much at will.

---

41 Thomas Corbishley, The Prayer of Jesus, Mowbray, 1976, p.20

That went on a few weeks. I had to be careful when to open up, because of disorientation on re-entry.

Eventually the sluice-gate closed; and though much else has happened since, I have never returned exactly to that place, nor would I expect to.

Through conversations since then, I have found out that epiphanies of this kind are quite common. Not identical, of course, for any two people.

But there may often be a sense of shocking realignment. Someone indoctrinated only in "nothing but" materialism could be very troubled by the unexpected onset of multi-dimensional reality. I was fortunate to be given, in childhood, a strong flexible "container" that enabled sudden unfolding to be welcomed.

However, maybe the only philosophy that can help us process such a happening "...is one that admits: when you have learned it all and lived it all thoroughly, you had better get ready to have it all collapse when you discover the highest wisdom is you know nothing."[42]

I certainly felt I knew nothing after the deluge described. Happily and serenely unhinged, I had not the slightest wish to be led into any "religious" explanation.

Nevertheless, encouraged by others, I did continue to re-connect, a bit hesitantly, with Christian worship in an Anglican environment. And it was not long before someone in authority there took me aside and asked if I was going to consider ordination. And so a path of potential service opened for me.

As part of preparation for that, before embarking on

---

42 Bernadette Roberts, The Experience of No-Self, State University of New York, 1993, p.121

formal training, I went to work in an Anglican cathedral. Lovable though the place was, I soon began to feel once again prison walls closing. However, not long after I began work there, the cathedral hosted a "Congress of Faiths."

The first speaker, when the Congress opened, was a Greek Orthodox bishop. Addressing assembled rabbis, imams, lamas and priests of every persuasion, he said: "Truth resides in the Greek Orthodox Church. My humble advice to you all is to join it."

But things got better. A rabbi who had been a survivor of Auschwitz spoke of the revelation, there, of idols of power and the dark side of the human soul. A Sufi imam gave a warmly-received talk on Muslim mystical practices. Purple-cassocked bishops, black-clad rabbis and saffron-robed lamas chatted amiably to one another as they queued at the Mothers' Union tea trolley.

But my best memory is of a man who was to become inspirational in my life, and who I encountered for the first time at the Congress. The Revd Dr Martin Israel was an Anglican priest, mystic and spiritual teacher. His own journey had been a complex one, from Judaism in his native South Africa via eastern and theosophical spiritualities to a profound acceptance of Christianity. He was a medical consultant, a pathologist, who thus represented Spirit in a hard-nosed and sceptical profession. And his gifts included powerful psychic awareness and clairvoyance, as I was later to discover.

Dr Israel led the Congress in an evening meditation, and took part in an interfaith panel during which he was asked a somewhat loaded question as to why he considered himself a Christian. I've never forgotten, and have always been grateful for, his answer: "...it is my dharma in this life to do this particular work. You can't be everything...The particular place where God has put me and the particular situation in which I work makes Christian witness the most suitable for me."[43]

The words look unexceptional now, reduced to print. But at that moment I almost wanted to weep. Here was someone offering a way through my confusion which was a way of Divine service that did not need to carry with it complete identification with this or that historical manifestation or institution.

Yes! Dharma! That was and is the key.

For you, too. Discover what your dharma is. Then follow it. You'll be shown how.

It won't necessarily be easy. But discover your dharma, discover how you are set up, pre-programmed, to serve in this life, and you'll very definitely be on the right track.

---

43 St Albans Congress of Faiths 1980, published transcript p.33

TEN

Hear, O Israel...

So... I was accepted for ordination, went off and studied for three years...and then worked in Church of England parishes, urban and (mostly) rural for the next thirty plus.

One morning when still young, walking to church as I did most days to say Matins and celebrate Holy Communion, I looked down at my black-shod feet striding along the pavement, and a strong realisation came over me: people I pass might presume this dog-collared figure on his way to church is in some way good. But I know, deep in my heart, I am not. God, who knows all things, knows I am not. That any outward show of holiness or knowledge or even common decency is play-acting, egoistic deception. God puts up with me, loves me even, but not because I am good. "No-one is good but God alone" (Luke 18:19).

The Sufi imam who had spoken at the Congress of Faiths had told his audience of "An-Nafs al-Ammarah," or "Nafs" for short, the primitive self, and how this devious imposter can dress itself up in apparent spiritual worthiness. The Prophet himself had once described the fight to dethrone this deceptive "Nafs" as "Jihad Akbar", the "big struggle."

Yet, as I looked at my feet walking along the pavement, I thought: Yes, I may be play-acting, but I am also, most sincerely, praying.

"You are here!" To this day, sometimes I shout this inwardly, as a call to attention. It reminds me of Mr Morgan, his exhortation to notice the moment. And then my heart with pleasure fills: once more, "everything feels alive, radiates energy, emanates Being."[44]

For me, the one addressed is usually the one who says, "Split a piece of wood; I am there. Lift up the stone, and you will find me there." (Gospel of Thomas: 77) And the one making the prayer is entwined, entangled, enmeshed with the "I Am" who describes his, her or itself as "the door." (John 10:9)

"No-one has seen God" said Martin Israel, when I first went to visit him; he had agreed to be my spiritual mentor shortly after my ordination. "Everything we say about God is inaccurate and probably wrong. But we can be *in touch* with God in silence, and this is *joy*."[45] He was articulating an ancient perception. I had already found out the truth of it some years before meeting Dr Israel, and was delighted to hear him say what he did, and wrote it down as soon as I got out into the street, hence my clear recollection of his exact wording and emphasis. I was thirty-two when I went to see him, newly immersed in a very public way of life as a minister of religion, gleaming white collar round my neck, well aware of my ludicrous unpreparedness to do what I was doing.

And yet, silence had unbolted the sluice for me. Once those floodgates open, nothing can be the same again. Even when the tide goes out, as it will, you know those waters will return, and that isn't some figment of your imagination but real.

Martin Israel continued to offer me spiritual accompaniment during my early years of ministry, and I am grateful

---

44 Eckhart Tolle, 1999, p.43
45 Martin Israel, private conversation with me, 18th October 1984

to this day for his counsel. He was a shy man. Arriving at his flat, however, I would usually pass a fellow-accompanee leaving, and the next person might ring the doorbell before he and I were done. In other words, Dr Israel was seeing a procession of people, and giving each of us his compassion and wisdom with the utmost energy and grace. What he said to me resonated deeply, and has done so ever since. He was truly a noble representative of the nation that has passed divine truth on down the ages, and whose name means "Wrestles with God."

I have been helped vastly, not only by Martin Israel and other explicit spiritual mentors but by numerous individuals I have met along the road. No human journey is possible alone. We accompany one another every step of the way. Even the most remote hermit still depends on the whole company of earth and heaven.

And meanwhile, the improvisation goes on. It never comes to an end: which is why "Stay awake" is so frequently what we're told, by Jesus and others.

ELEVEN

You shall love

So, at the end of all that, what am I supposed to say about this originating mystery, "the Lord our God," who Jesus commands us to love?

"Silence is the essence" said Dr Israel, "in silence we are actually in contact with God. The Holy Spirit works through our quiet mind."[46] He was rightly suspicious of pictures, definitions, fixed ideas.

Nevertheless, we imagine in certain ways people we claim to know. We are well aware our picture of x or y isn't the whole story or even a bit of it. But we have a name to hold onto and a sense of what it feels like to be with such and such a person.

Throughout this book I am happily using the word presence to describe a sense I have had from childhood of a profound creative essence or power that may be glimpsed or accessed, whose effect is energizing and full of wonder. That is what I imagine I am in touch with.

But knowing this phenomenon has at least something to do with unknowing what we think we know.

As described above, I was initiated in a strong religious tradition. We learnt catechism questions and answers by rote from an early age, and I can remember the nun asking

---

46 Private conversation with me, 18th October 1984

74

"Where is God?" and all of us little children chanting back, "God is everywhere."

Everywhere! The thought of that really amazed me at the time. As far away as it was possible to be. And yet right up close, here and now.

The thought still amazes me now. "You are here!" I say. In my hand I am holding a pebble from the seashore, pitted and speckled with hundreds of marks. I imagine each spot to represent a galaxy, itself containing trillions of whirling suns and planets, between them the silence and mystery of deep space.

I sit here staring at the pebble. It was rolling in the foam for millennia, until I randomly picked it up one afternoon. There are limitless similar pebbles. And this dimension we are temporarily in, of stars and planets, is one universe among, for all we know, countless others.

So, where in all that is God?

Everywhere, according to the Bible. "Where can I go from your spirit? Or where can I flee from your presence? If I ascend to heaven, you are there; if I make my bed in Sheol, you are there. If I take the wings of the morning and settle at the farthest limits of the sea, even there your hand shall lead me, and your right hand shall hold me fast..."(Psalm 139: 7–10).

In primeval collisions of stars. In a tiny shoot reaching out towards its sun through the gravels of some remote planet. And right here on my desk.

Root and crown of complexity. Beyond unknowable: "En Soph".

Yet, as the author of the "Cloud of Unknowing" put it, "By love may He be getyn and holden..."

Amazingly, I find that to be so.

The term "Father" is of course hallowed by Jesus' use of it. But like much spiritual imagery, "Father" is a figure of speech, even if powerfully so for Jesus. Connection with what I encounter as presence doesn't really, to me, feel much like relationship with a human parent. Spiritual metaphors have their usefulness, especially early on, but we don't need to push them too hard or take them too literally.

Our father or mother is one with whom we are connected, for good or ill, whose genes are part of us and whose blood flows in our veins. Nothing, absolutely nothing whatsoever, can change that. Any half-decent human mother or father continues to love and care about her or his children, no matter what. "Are not two sparrows sold for a penny?" Jesus said, "Yet not one of them will fall to the ground unperceived by your Father. And even the hairs of your head are all counted" (Matthew 10: 29, 30). The metaphor is meant to reveal entanglement: not some impersonal "first cause", but supra-rational love.

Yet such love can sometimes, in practice, feel like abandonment. "My God, my God, why have you forsaken me?" is often the cry not only of Jesus Christ but of faithful people everywhere.

I have been sustained, however, by the divine persona Christians name "The Holy Spirit" (another metaphor): compass of truth, dancing like sun glitter over the ocean.

That's how it is for me, or at least, that's how it is for me today. For you it will be different.

TWELVE

...with all your heart

A child runs to her mother, hugs her, cosies up in her mother's lap and remains there a good long time. Nothing is said, nothing needs to be. The child isn't asking for anything. The event barely qualifies as a happening that could be described in words.

Those who sat and gazed at the Sacrament during "Expositions" that took place when I was little, mostly just sat there. Our cat, when she climbs up onto me and goes to sleep, isn't expecting to be played with or fed. She just trusts I'm not going to throw her off.

"What is the first commandment?" asked the scribe, "How do you live a truly good life?" "Love God with your whole heart" was the first part of Jesus' response. According to the gospels, Jesus himself, to the mystification of those around him, often went to a quiet place "and there he prayed." (Mark 1:35)

If you had been able to watch him, what might you have seen?

"Prayer," for most of my life, has been an off-putting word. It has meant hypocritical, stale or defunct religiosity. Or it has suggested something most people don't feel competent to do.

I was intrigued, once my blockages had been removed, by what the prayer of Jesus, alone in the Galilean darkness, might have been. Not, surely, formal devotion: all that sort of activity would have happened out loud, in public. No, surely Jesus was connecting with the one he called his "Abba," heart to heart.

And such connection maybe was the wellspring of his life.

So, encouraged by Dr Israel, but also drawn by desire, I began as a young adult to try to make time at the beginning of every day to "touch base" with the mystery. And that has continued. It was difficult when my children were young and I was under many work obligations. Latterly, it has become much easier.

Were you able to watch me, all you would see would be someone sitting on a wooden chair, appearing to do nothing.

But I have already done the difficult bit by then: to be in that place at that time. Just by getting out of bed, I join with all the others who at that moment are Earth's praying contingent. And by opening up to silence, I touch base... like the daughter hugging her mother and being hugged back.

Some sort of exchange seems to me to happen. Mostly, it's barely something one could describe in words.

I don't, at least to begin with, ask for anything. Very occasionally, an event might occur, such as that alluded to by St Paul: "...that very Spirit intercedes with sighs too deep for words" (Romans 8:26): as though Paul was being prayed-through, "channelling" the life-giving Spirit.

But such happenings are rare, at any rate in my earthbound experience. More normal is what Buddhists call the "monkey mind" chattering on, daydreams, snippets of conversation, worries. I've gradually learnt to let much of that pass, not to try to stop it; just the top of my brain doing what the brain does. Proves I'm alive! But I pay as little attention as possible to it: like flotsam floating by on the river.

In any case, the life-giving instruction here is: love God "with your whole heart." That isn't just a turn of phrase.

Your heart, in spiritual as in everyday imagery, is not merely the extraordinary organ that pumps blood round your body, marvellous though that is. "Heart" refers to the centre of yourself, normally imagined as located in the depths of your chest though not coterminous with the physical heart.

You will be aware that your "gross" (!) physical body is a stupendously complex creation. (I was never a medical student, but when training for ordained ministry, as part of a hospital placement I got to watch a post-mortem examination. I was amazed by the subtlety of even a deceased, dissected human body, and how each part depends on, and in turn empowers, all the other parts).

Yet, in addition to the marvels of sight, hearing, digestion, our bodies are eco-systems of energy. You'll know that, if you have undergone reflexology or acupuncture. Such inherited patterns of receptivity and memory and wisdom are mapped in varying but complementary ways in pictures that come to us from east and west.

For instance, the system of seven Chakras or energy centres in Indian cosmology describes the Heart Chakra, Anahata, as bridge between the downward pull of material life and the transcendence of spirit. Comparable in western Kabbalah is Tiphareth, the Heart Sefirah: this too is portrayed as the all-important intersection between vital energies of earth and those of heaven.

The point is, when I say, "I know in my heart," marvellous and vital though the fleshy pump is, it's not that I'm referring to.

So, if you wish to taste Jesus' advice about loving God with your heart, you need, first of all, to get there: out of your head and into your heart.

"Proceeding in this way you will smooth for yourself a true and straight path...which is the following: the mind should be in the heart...and thence, from the depths of the heart, offer up prayers to God...When the mind, there within the heart, at last tastes and sees that the Lord is good, and delights therein...it will no longer wish to leave this place in the heart..."[47] St Simeon, one of the revered teachers of prayer within Orthodox Christianity, wrote those words a thousand years ago. I have experienced them to be true.

Or here is an equally revered, twentieth century Hindu philosopher, Sri Aurobindo: "The psychic being" (by which he means inner nature, often referred to as the soul) "is in the heart centre in the middle of the chest (not in the physical heart, for all the centres are in the middle of the body), but it is deep behind...it is felt as if one is going deep down till one reaches that central place...The more one goes, the more intense becomes the psychic happiness..."[48]

What those teachers are describing is a practice of centring in quite a precise physical location, "deep behind" the middle of the chest, and "loving" from there. That, for

---

47 St Simeon the New Theologian, quoted in Jacob Needleman, Lost Christianity, Element, 1990, p.160

48 Sri Aurobindo, The Integral Yoga, Sri Aurobindo Ashram Trust, 1993, p.206

me, is comparable to the picture I gave of the little girl with her mother.

You can focus your attention in other parts of your body, notably your gut, known as hara in Japanese martial arts. That has to do with "lower" instinctual energies, and I will touch on hara when we come to Jesus' advice about loving God with your whole strength. "If we exclude the hara" says American psychotherapist John J. Prendergast, "our spiritual quest can become arid and lifeless."[49]

But our purpose in focusing on the heart is, not only does it represent deep centre but intersection: between hara and all that it represents (groundedness, sexuality, bowels, earth) and supposedly "higher" energies (order, imagination, intellect), with a clear path leading from there across the void into divine sunlight and the great unknown. Or, to say it another way, to be in one's heart is not to be in one's head, where we tittle-tattle much of our time away and from which attempts are sometimes made to sustain emotionally threadbare "faith", usually with unhelpful results.

One of the reasons Christian "faith" has become a dead letter for many of my contemporaries is that it can appear aridly mental, "excarnate,"[50] unhydrated by any life-giving energies of earth or heaven. But that doesn't seem to be how Christ was originally experienced. "The water that I will give" said Jesus "will become...a spring of water gushing up to eternal life" (John 4:14). Such phrases were not just figures of speech. They refer to something people felt and knew.

---

49 John J.Prendergast, The Deep Heart, Sounds True, 2019, p.135
50 Charles Taylor, A Secular Age, Belknap,2007, p.288

I say that with certainty, since there have been times I have felt and known it too.

Not continuously; and one does not go consciously seeking this or that feeling. The command is to love, that alone. We might say, to touch base. So how do we do it?

Breathing is the classic vehicle of prayer or of any sort of meditation. You become aware of your breathing; no need to breathe differently from normal: you just notice your breath, as though it were the tide washing in. And as you notice where the breath originates, you mentally position yourself there: and that's the centre of your being, your heart: from which you are conscious of your bowels and genitalia and limbs, also of your upper regions, mouth and eyes and ears, and the brain, where thoughts continually bob past, like paper boats on the river.

There may be a sense of void, vastness and alienation... but it is towards a magnetic hum of light that I find myself drawn. According to Christian templates, this is what St Paul mentions as "Christ in you, the hope of glory" (Colossians 1:27)...that infinite "I Am" permeating my own small "I am"... my heart one with the heart of being.

When the little vessel that is my heart opens like a secret doorway, it sometimes feels as though sweetness flows in. Where is God? God is everywhere, including here, knowing me with my fears and worries and preoccupations, and flooding me with light.

But there is nothing systematic about any of the above.

Tides come and go. Everyone who prays encounters periods of so-called "dryness". When Jesus cried out dramatically from the cross "My God, my God...," he was quoting a Psalm of ancient Israel that expresses the alienation, not just of him but of everyone. Maybe his heart-connection with his Abba was volatile at other moments: in the extreme circumstance of Gethsemane we read that "his sweat became like great drops of blood falling down on the ground."(Luke 22:44)

Fortunately, those of us who are mere foot soldiers don't encounter that sort of drama, just the occasional episode of boredom or distractedness.

But what I am describing is a relationship, which is why it can't be exactly predicted. My part is to be willing to love, to go down into my heart and wait for whatever happens, and give of my honest truth.

Why? Because I want to touch base with what is real. Because I have it in me to do that, to be part of the praying contingent of the universe. Because my heart seems designed to open in that way. And because it appears to be my "dharma."

The above is an account of what loving God with my whole heart means to me. I can't predict what the phrase would mean to you, nor do I know what your dharma is. Only you can find that out.

The imagery we use is just imagery in the end, even including the mighty word "God." All such images are culturally conditioned, produced out of our imagination. That doesn't mean they're not true. They point to a reality that can't necessarily be said in words, but can be known at times, touched (in silence, as Martin Israel and many others have said) and channelled in non-verbal ways, such as via music.

Elsewhere, I've named that phenomenon as presence.

THIRTEEN

...with all your soul

We have something of the divine in us, amid all the neurons, guts and shit.

There is no word used more randomly or imprecisely than "soul." But what the multifarious meanings of the word seem to have in common is that they are all about a greater, wider or deeper sense of who I am.

To love God with your whole soul is to love with all you are, not merely with your personality or your ego.

When I was at my long-ago Catholic primary school, we were given a picture of the soul as some kind of mystical blob within us. That blob was forever becoming "stained" by sin (our childish misdemeanours) and was in danger of being killed altogether if we did something really wicked, such as absent ourselves from Mass on Sunday. The way the doctrine was taught, as though soulcraft was some invisible version of chemistry or mechanical engineering, made perfect sense to an eight-year-old.

But as I and my contemporaries grew, we considered what we had been indoctrinated into was nonsense. Unfortunately that meant awareness of "soul" went the same way as other childish toys and comics: not transcended or included, but binned.

What I was left with was a brave new materialist persona, fashionably sceptical. Secretly I doubted that identity, and sought forms of self-initiation in nature and through music.

Near where I worked in central London, the supposedly "lost" River Fleet, concreted over centuries before, still ran on its way to the Thames and to the ocean; once, when workmen had opened a storm drain cover, I saw and heard and smelt it, roaring in its deep subterraneous gulley: a living reality, forgotten, unknown.

In a comparable way my soul still seemed real, however much friends might mock or rubbish.

It took an incoming tide, not of floodwater but of transforming light, to break open the materialist pretence and drown it in wonder. The little word "wonder," in both senses, noun and verb, continues to describe what aerates my life.

We have something of the divine in us, amid all the neurons, guts and shit.

Even more astonishingly, there is potentially something of us, every single half-witted screwed up shitty blundering bozo of us, in the divine.

That we "may become participants of the divine nature" (2 Peter: 4) is an ancient aspiration of Christian faith. Sometimes called "Koinonia", or Communion, it is anticipated and mimicked in the Christian sacrament of that name, every repetition of which is called in my tradition a Celebration.

But many people over the centuries have considered it blasphemous to imagine we flawed creatures might draw near to divine majesty in any such way. "For my thoughts are not your thoughts, nor are your ways my ways, says the Lord. For as the heavens are higher than the earth, so are my ways higher than your ways, and my thoughts than your thoughts."(Isaiah 55: 8, 9)

And the (Kabbalistic) Jewish myth "Tzimtzum," mentioned earlier, imagines "exile as an element in God himself..." which for Jewish people "was the most powerful and seductively appropriate of symbols."[51]

That's the sense, so often repeated, of life here on earth as "all fuckin' shit", "My God, my God, why have you forsaken me?" (Psalm 22:1) cried across an empty abyss, or into seemingly "indifferent immensity".

Both the attitudes described above seem to me congruent with reality.

To assume salvation without any grounding in the tragedy, muck, injustice and stupidity of life, and without self-examination or attempt at metanoia, seems at best a half-baked exercise. As church religion here in England has had to sell itself more and more as a "feelgood" commodity, so it has become more dependent on facile triumphalism without the historic ingredients of doubt, contrition or lament.

On the other hand, for reasons expounded at length above, the nihilist orthodoxy seems to me equally facile, because it denies and tries to airbrush away the inner and outer light people have always witnessed. Openness to possibility can lead to wonder, in both its senses.

All that, and much more, is part of the territory expressed in the little word "soul."

To love with your whole soul is to love with all you are.

All you are is more than your ego or personality,

---

51 Gershom Scholem, trans.Ralph Manheim, On the Kabbalah and its Symbolism, Schocken, 1969, p.113

outward (and quite possibly beautiful) symptoms here in this present field of existence. "Soul" in my understanding relates to an identity more mysterious, and more capacious, than our present mode of reality.

It's not that I have a soul. It's that my soul has me. And participates in presence: for which we may use the baggage-laden shorthand "God."

"And you, my soul, I found again...where I least expected you. You climbed out of a dark shaft. You announced yourself to me in dreams...You let me see truths of which I had no previous inkling. You let me undertake journeys, whose endless length would have scared me, if the knowledge of them had not been secure in you."[52]

"Soul holds the knowledge of what we individually were born to do and to be."[53] It may show up through what feels an insistent call: the call might seem frustratingly unspecific at times, though it will certainly be uniquely you-shaped. It may, or may not, readily translate into "vocation."

For instance, the call I received in a variety of different ways seemed to have to do with acknowledgement of the (deeply unfashionable) divine, with being a "dancer before God" (anyone who has known me personally might shudder at that concept!) In my circumstances, the call got translated into a localised expression of Christian priesthood.

The translation was rough, the fit not always good. My uneventful life, nonetheless, was given some usefulness and focus. I was able to offer service, however poorly.

---

52 C.G.Jung, The Red Book, trans. Mark Kyburz, John Peck, Sonu Shamdasani, W.W.Norton, 2009, p.131
53 Bill Plotkin, Wild Mind, New World Library, 2013, p.25

And it is service that can open, for each of us in a particular way, a window onto soul. Whereas to go down into your heart is (figuratively) to travel inward, soul is outward-facing. To love God with one's soul is to love the God who "is everywhere", who is present in all the other souls, and who says "Split a piece of wood; I am there. Lift up the stone, and you will find me there" (Gospel of Thomas:77).

So-called "psychic" faculties are aptitudes of the soul. Those "whose minds are still and attentive" wrote my late mentor Martin Israel, "will be aware of greater psychic communication from those round them, and...from the world beyond the grave."[54]

There can be no rigid demarcation: body and soul are porous, one to another. When I was with Martin Israel I sometimes felt he was discreetly scanning me, taking a kind of internal x-ray that would help him "read" me, as it were, soul to soul. In infancy one of my children would sometimes respond aloud to thoughts I had not spoken: troubling to a child, but a valuable aptitude in a caring adult.

Your soul might reach out further. You might, for instance, experience subtle connections with places and the lives and traces of lives they contain.

"The Australian aborigines" writes Bill Plotkin "say that for each person there is one place in the natural world where he most belongs, a place that's part of him and where he is part of that place. In finding that place, he also finds his true self."[55] Thus, in some inexplicable way, you might "remember the future": I did, when first

---

54 Martin Israel, Summons to Life, Hodder and Stoughton, 1974, p.99.
55 Bill Plotkin, Soulcraft, New World Library, 2003, p.40

visiting a region I would eventually go to live thirty years later.

Unlocking your soul might also lead to discovery of the ground of your being in animal and other wild kingdoms. For Christians the obvious exemplar is Francis of Assisi, most beloved of saints. "In stories of his life, Francis is quoted as talking to or about larks, lambs, rabbits, pheasants, falcons, cicadas, waterfowl, bees, the famous wolf of Gubbio, pigs...He addresses inanimate creation too, as if it were ensouled...his 'Canticle of the Creatures' includes fire, wind, water, Brother Sun, Sister Moon, and, of course, our 'sister mother earth' herself."[56]

Taking that further, "...you may have fleeting visions of water, stones, Co-Walkers or Allies, plants, animals. These...often arise as an affinity for, or deep sense of, Air, Fire, Water, Earth, Sky Above, or Land Below."[57]

Such soul-devotion to Earth and her creatures is completely normal, and has indeed powerfully increased here in the West during the plastic and concrete epoch in which I have lived. Nature mysticism, described as such or simply thought of as gardening, has become a remedial spirituality, flourishing in my lifetime as other forms of religion have shrunk.

Such love has never been more necessary, as we humans continue in other ways to trash the planet.

Then again your soul-antennae might be receptive to signals from further reaches or wavelengths of existence (all words in this area are of course metaphorical). "In my Father's house" Jesus tells us in John's gospel "there are many dwelling places" (John 14: 2). The dwelling-places will

---

56 Richard Rohr, Eager to Love, Franciscan Media, 2014, p.46
57 R.J.Stewart, The Well of Light, R.J.Stewart Books, 2004, p.43

be indiscernible to physical sense but sometimes glimpsed here and now through openness to our souls' gifts.

They include human post-mortem regions, pictured in a variety of ways. I heard much in childhood from the Catholic side of my family about so-called "souls in Purgatory", for whom we were exhorted to pray. One of my great-aunts seemed in possession of a detailed schedule of her late husband's progress through those corrective regions.

Meanwhile on the Protestant side, my paternal grandparents, who had lived, fought and nursed through two great wars, were spiritualists, communing with deceased friends, and, after my grandmother's death, seemingly with one another.

Any such intercession or communication has to acknowledge that words are physical things being utilized to describe the non-physical.

However, there is evidence to assert "a spectrum of worlds"[58] beyond human death. Martin Israel spoke to me occasionally of his remedial intercessory work with and for beings, most of them strangers. He seemed to consider that work an obligation put upon him, burdensome but somehow part of his dharma. "In psychical communication" he wrote "there is an apparently direct contact from the deepest layer of consciousness of one person to another; it is from soul to soul."[59] In a less exalted way I too have occasionally known similar contact.

And the "many dwelling places" are not limited to human souls but refer also to beings nearly beyond our ability to

---

58 Stafford Betty, Heaven and Hell Unveiled, White Crow Books, 2014, p.13

59 Martin Israel, The Spirit of Counsel, Hodder and Stoughton, 1983, p.69

comprehend, though not quite: "Such, therefore" wrote Pseudo-Dionysus in the fifth century "are they who participate first...in the Divine Mysteries. Wherefore they, above all, are pre-eminently worthy of the name Angel, because they first receive the Divine Light..."[60]

For all the grandeur of that description, angels and we human bozos seem quite capable of developing intimate friendships. I have heard improbable people speak movingly of their encounters with angels.

"Therefore" wrote Valentin Tomberg, "think of your guardian Angel...when you have problems, questions to resolve, tasks to accomplish, plans to formulate, cares and fears to appease! Think of him as a luminous cloud of maternal love above you, moved by the sole desire to serve you and be useful to you..."[61]

Not only angels but beings from unfamiliar frequencies are sometimes encountered and spoken of; but "the nature of the subtle realms is so relational that no-one else's map, however well drawn and detailed, will be the same as your own...Your map is a description of your relationships. Someone else's description, while potentially helpful in some regards, may lead you astray if you try to apply it literally to your own experiences."[62]

All the above is merely to illustrate that our souls face outward, and that relationship is possible across a wide range of territory. More potent than any esoteric aptitude, however, is openness of you and me, capacious souls as we are, to the grace and wisdom of God the Holy Spirit.

---

60 Pseudo-Dionysus: The Celestial Hierarchies, trans. Anon., Shrine of Wisdom, 1935, p.33

61 Meditations on the Tarot, p.379

62 David Spangler, Subtle Worlds, Lorian, 2010, p.64

Her touch will have a transformative effect, as expressed in famous words of St Paul: "...the fruit of the Spirit is love, joy, peace, patience, kindness, generosity, faithfulness, gentleness and self-control. There is no law against such things...Let us not become conceited, competing against one another, envying one another" (Galatians 5: 22–23, 26).

If only we could be soul-directed in such a way! If only we could become ourselves!

Someone who became herself, in the darkest of times, was the Jewish Dutchwoman Etty Hillesum. As a young adult she found herself in the throes of the Nazi occupation of her country.

"They are merciless, totally without pity" she wrote. "And we must be all the more merciful ourselves. That's why I prayed early this morning: 'O God, times are too hard for frail people like myself. I know that a new and kinder day will come. I would so much like to live on, if only to express all the love I carry within me. And there is only one way of preparing the new age, by living it even now in our hearts. Somewhere in me I feel so light, without the least bitterness and so full of strength and love. I would so much like to help prepare the new age.'"[63]

How could Etty Hillesum write with such iridescent tenderness at such a hellish moment? Aged 27, she volunteered to go to a Nazi transit camp at Westerbork, believing she could help her fellow-Jews. From there, she was inevitably deported to the horrors of Auschwitz. The Nazis managed to kill her young body. But they could do nothing about her luminous soul, which radiates to this day through letters and diaries she left behind her.

Of course, those Nazis were souls too, as Etty would

---

63 Etty Hillesum, op.cit., pp.226–7

have been the first to say. They had been beguiled and seduced by a glamorous Nationalist-Socialist thought-form which enslaved them and all around them. Such energies, known as egregores[64] in Jewish-Christian tradition and as tulpas and tulkus in Tibetan Buddhism, are autonomous psychic viruses arising from and sustained by human thought and belief. Egregores and the counter-inspiration they engender can be seen not only with hindsight but possibly in events happening in your own world right now.

Once created, a psychic virus, like a physical one, is tough to eradicate. According to some, it may be "home or conduit for a specific psychic intelligence of a nonhuman nature connecting the invisible dimensions with the material world in which we live."[65]

Valentin Tomberg, who had lived through the terrors first of Bolshevism then of Nazism, wrote: "We people of the twentieth century know that the 'great pests' of our time are the Egregores of 'ideological superstructures,' which have cost humanity more life and suffering than the great epidemics of the Middle Ages."[66]

The very freedom made possible through non-interference of the divine, "Tzimtzum", becomes freedom for such localised deities to arise in all their beguiling certainty. They are the very idols warned against in the ancient Jewish Commandments: "You shall not bow down to them or worship them." (Exodus 20: 5)

Such thought-forms are not only large, sinuous entanglements like Nazism. They may be seen in everyday form within families, culture, businesses and human systems of all kinds: churches, for instance, bristle with

---

64 (Pronounced "eager-gors")
65 Mark Stavish, Egregores, Inner Traditions, 2018, p.3
66 Meditations on the Tarot, p.409

them. Presumably they are a necessity of earthly life, as are physical viruses. Not all are harmful. The commandment accepts their reality, but says (and says it in no uncertain terms): do not do them obeisance.

Easier said than done, especially when confronted by large, coercive, terrifying power. What Etty Hillesum and others have shown is that the only sure way to retain one's sovereignty in the presence of such terror is by love.

Hillesum was not "godly" in any outward manner her contemporaries would have recognized. But she was unwilling to give way to hatred of her oppressors, because she saw divine light, buried but still latent in their mangled souls. "The terrifying thing" she wrote on 27th February 1942 "is that systems grow too big for men and hold them in a satanic grip, the builders no less than the victims of the system."[67]

I would love to fill this chapter with more quotations from Etty Hillesum: I won't, but urge you to read her memoir for yourself. Her light shines on.

To love with your whole soul is to be fully present: heart, mind and strength, imagination and spiritual being. It is to give of yourself freely.

Service to people or animals or other living creatures unleashes our souls: hence the joy so many discover in volunteering.

To love God with your whole soul: what a ride that would be! What would be the "God" towards which such love might be directed? No sectarian deity could possibly suffice.

"You are here!" Sometimes I shout that inwardly, as a call to attention. It reminds me of Mr Morgan long ago, his

---

67 Etty Hillesum, op.cit., p.105

exhortation to notice the moment. And then my heart with pleasure fills: once more, "...everything feels alive, radiates energy, emanates Being."[68]

To be aware that presence, origin (whether imagined personally or not) is here, now, in this place, in this encounter has always, always had for me a transformative effect: meditation in action, without pretentious piety. It has made me less fearful, more courageous, more relaxed, kinder, happier...pretty much instantly. Such openness to "God" in the moment has been one of the most joyful spiritual practices of my life.

To open in that way assumes a certain "unknowing". I am just aware of my own connection, in the ignorant way a child knows her own mother.

That's how I love God with my soul...some of the time... when I remember.

But you must find out who your soul is and how your soul loves...only you can find that out, no-one can do it for you.

Here are some words by St Bonaventure, thirteenth-century biographer of Francis of Assisi: "The soul itself is an image of God, to which God is so present that the soul can actually grasp God, and 'is capable of possessing God and of being a partaker in God.'"[69]

Amen to that.

---

68 Eckhart Tolle, op.cit., p.43
69 Bonaventure, Itinerarium,3,2 (quoting Augustine, De Trinitate). In Richard Rohr, op.cit., p.80

FOURTEEN

...with all your mind

What are your earliest memories? How do you recall them? What do they look, sound, smell, feel like? Where were you when those images were implanted in your mind?

I was born a few years after the Second World War, and my immediate environment was marked by its wounds and damage. Men and women walked about sullenly, in what seemed even to a child a careworn world, so much so I remember being astonished when my father told me one day we, the British, had actually been on the winning side of the war that was always being spoken of with such disquiet. My grandparents, with whom we lived, had rescued a dog that had survived its home's destruction in the Blitz (there were, as mentioned earlier, numerous ruined houses, "bomb sites", near where we lived). This dog would, so they said, give them early warning of an imminent bombing raid by cowering in terror under furniture, long before any air-raid sirens went off: "She could hear the enemy planes crossing the channel", I was told (we lived many miles from that sea).

There were respites from the gloom. We were fortunate to have a garden, where my green-fingered Gran nurtured vegetables and flowers and the grasses she especially loved. These were left to grow long, to show off their many-seeded heads, and among my earliest memories are blissful times passed lying amidst their perfume, gazing up at racing clouds and wondering how far the sky reached.

My parents had both served in the Navy, but after the war they had become actors, and had met on stage in the north of England. Dad was able to continue his acting career for a while after I was born, but Mum was stuck upstairs in her parents' house with a baby...not what she had dreamt of. Among my earliest memories is Mum singing round the rooms with romantic flair and passion, throwing her long black hair about as she sang. The numbers performed, for me and our pet budgerigar in the otherwise bare rooms, were from American musicals, new at the time. Sometimes I remember there were tears.

Who or what is the "me" that remembers these things? Who is the "you" that recalls your memories, whatever they are? To be conscious of being conscious: this is part of the territory into which we are venturing, as we explore Jesus' invitation to love God "with your whole mind."

What does my mind do, what is it for?

It stores, processes and continually interprets massive quantities of memory, much of it beneath the surface of everyday awareness.

It notices, logs and categorizes the immediate environment and happenings of the moment. It gives attention to anything that might trigger alarm. It reacts to and reflects upon feelings, needs, evidence right now; and can easily be wounded. There were many traumatized minds around when I was little.

It worries about futures. It spins stories, fantasizes. It weaves simulacra of experiences and events in words. It studies, identifies, names, lists and interprets evidence. It unfolds abstract languages of number, symbol and sound not only to weigh and measure actual universes but to devise parallel new ones.

You know all that, and there is much more that could

be added. We are told, by people who claim expertise in these matters, that an enormous proportion of what our minds do is programmed, instinctual. Certainly in almost every respect our mental activity is shared and inherited and collaborative and connected. I am writing words here, you are reading. Neither of us invented them.

All the above is blindingly obvious, but I would like to underline one feature maybe less commonly emphasised, which is that I am aware of the mental activity within and around me, or at any rate some of it.

I am.

I am able to stand outside the turning, instinctual, agonising, reflecting mind and observe its machinations.

I am: aware that I am aware[70].

In the antique symbolism of Kabbalah, the "Tree of Life" introduced earlier, there are two left-side branches that express some of this. Geburah, or "Severity," has to do with judgement, with boundaries and laws, including those of nature and physics and the widely-accepted Hindu-Buddhist concept Karma ("actions have consequences"). Geburah is truth, the "sweet spot" of justice which in practice is so difficult to discern.

Beneath it, Hod, or "Splendour", can represent the very business of discernment: words, numbers, pattern-making, story-weaving, ongoing glories of creativity which we humans so exuberantly share. Geburah and Hod, like all branches on the "Tree", symbolize ways in which divine and human permeate one another. Mind is pictured, not only as a vital part of being human, but as a key embodiment of the mystery of our divine connectedness.

---

70 For an illuminating exposition of this, see Rupert Spira, Being Aware of Being Aware, Sahaja, 2017.

So, taking account of the above and many other ways "mind" manifests...what might it mean to love God with your whole mind?

When I was in my late twenties, I passed a Church of England selection conference and was sent to study at a Theological College so that a few years later I might be ordained into the Church's professional ministry. The College had a library housed in a gallery whose large windows overlooked a garden. The place always seemed morning-bright. There were thousands upon thousands of books, stacked up to the ceiling: products of extraordinary minds searching for truth across centuries of human experience.

I had a strong desire, when first there, to swallow the place and all its contents whole. I wanted to eat it all, to consume it, to gobble it up, so starved did I feel of intellectual nourishment in the pursuit of God.

Theology is no more a single subject than history or psychology: diverse areas of thought were represented in the College library, among them philosophy, biblical studies of many and varied kinds, ethical and pastoral endeavours, doctrine, its history and development, shelves of argumentation about "other faiths," and much else.

I loved it all, and sailed through essays, dissertations and exams, propelled by a gale of enthusiasm. I'd finally discovered something I could do.

But shortcomings became apparent when I was ordained, and went to serve as curate in a large not very affluent parish, where people struggled with the usual problems of daily life. I could "fillet" a complicated biblical text, as we had been taught, and explain what the Greek meant, and come up with propositional answers to questions people weren't asking. On rare occasions that might have helped someone. But mostly it didn't.

One useful subject we had learnt a little about, towards the end of my time at college, was listening. To give attention to another person, to listen fully, patiently and respectfully, proved more valuable, at street level, than most of the theology under the sun.

Yet we humans are born with outsize heads, there to house capacious brains. Our stupendous brains are in turn generating and receiving apparatuses for the reasoning, inventing, seeking, analysing, extemporizing, measuring, feeling, delving, codifying, contesting, enlightening, collaborative phenomenon we call mind. That is a gift from God: surely one of the very greatest.

To dismiss the contents of the theological library I once inhabited as merely cerebral, as if the cerebrum is unimportant, would be ridiculous. Perhaps less absurd might be to argue theologians and divines have been trying to capture a fish which either long since eluded them, or was never possible to be netted in the first place.

What I thought I was doing when studying theology was exploring the tradition into which I had been inducted, while also seeking truth "right here right now." The library I wished to devour mostly contained mental and spiritual wrangling from within the Christian universe.

I have sometimes imagined Christianity as a mighty estuary made up of numbers of rivulets and currents all heading in roughly the same direction but by numerous serpentine courses, with shifting sandbanks strewn with ancient wrecks and other hidden hazards. Every part of this estuary is considered the mainstream by those sailing it; and while Christians are alleged to love one another, mind-boggling levels of ignorance, fear and prejudice separate those navigating one part of the river from those on another. Egregores, see above, thrive and abound, enveloping people within their all-explaining and often toxic systems.

To love God with your whole mind, however, must be to cut free from any such closed framework of obedience. Whichever way we contemplate divine oneness, it can only signify infinity: the ocean into which all rivers flow. When they enter that limitless sea, the individual streams surrender their temporary identity.

We need not abandon the ground we stand on just yet: but it seems to me good to recognise the provisional nature of any human set-up, however inspired.

The egregores I have lived with since those student days have often been secular ones: management ("be the best you can be"), money, national or corporate identity. I am beyond grateful to have lived in a time of materialistic science (especially medicine, without which I would by now be a blind toothless cripple).

But despite growing old, part of me is still a child lying in the sweet summer grass, wondering how far the sky reaches. The one loved with my whole mind "is everywhere", not merely in a single officially authorized designation. To quote Thomas yet again, "Split a piece of wood; I am there. Lift up the stone, and you will find me there." Eluding any of our human nets. Discoverable, afresh, this day.

So, how is Christ present to the mind of a suicide bomber? Or to the lust of a rapist? What sort of deity permits predation, on which earthly life depends?

Is so-called "creation" not, as that old man with his pramload of junk complained, "all fuckin' shit", at least quite a lot of the time?

There is, unquestionably, something in Jacques Monod's words about the seeming "indifferent immensity" of the universe.

But then, mixed up in what seems toxic or indifferent, a glimmer of presence is glimpsed. "The light shines in the darkness" wrote St John, "and the darkness did not overcome it" (John 1:5).

When Jesus went into dark places to commune with one he called Abba, his monkey-mind must have kept on chattering. He was, after all, human, like us.

But what cousin Jesus did in the darkness was go aside from the chatter. We are aware we are aware. We can stand momentarily outside the verbal and instinctual chatter, view all that from outside, as though it were a stream passing. We can focus our attention, instead, on something other.

For me as a child at "Exposition", the something other was a white circle of unleavened bread within its radiate monstrance. For a rambler today, it might be wind-thrashed trees, or a distant valley bathed in sunlight. For religionists it could be an icon or sacred image, for people of (whichever) book some word or phrase of scripture. The object of meditation serves as cat flap from one world into another. It opens a new folder of mind, and the everyday is temporarily banished to a backroom.

What your mind has power to do for short spells is maintain attention. That is your presence, the presence of your heart, soul, mind and strength, your "I am" squinting towards infinite "I Am."

As anyone knows, attention is one thing to write about, another to do. Not only does the monkey keep chattering: the chatter may become seductive.

FOURTEEN

A practice called Centering Prayer, followed by many people, recommends a simple word or phrase, not so much an object of meditation as an anchor, to hold us fast whenever riptides of distraction threaten to sweep us away. The practice was derived from the medieval "Cloud of Unknowing", quoted earlier, whose author tells you to "fasten this worde to thin heart...This worde schal be thi scheeld and thi speere..."[71]

One of those who taught and developed Centering Prayer in my lifetime was the Cistercian monk Thomas Keating. He wrote: "The sacred word is only a gesture... it has no meaning other than your intention... it establishes an interior climate that facilitates the movement of faith in the divine presence within."[72]

So, with the help of a sacred word or image, or maybe simply giving attention to your breath, sink down towards your heart, leaving your mind (chattering, fantasizing) temporarily unattended upstairs.

To love God with your mind is to consent, surrender, allow God to know your heart. However that might be. Whatever form, or un-form, that might take.

You do what you do, your mind consents to it...not only as you alone but as one of a galaxy of praying hearts throughout creation, coming into and out of focus every second until the end of time.

That is how creation breathes: and you for a few brief moments are part of it.

And it is real.

---

71 Op. Cit., p.38
72 Thomas Keating, Open Mind, Open Heart, Continuum, 2006, p.40

You may be playing, pretending; but the thing is really happening.

You are praying.

FIFTEEN

...with all your strength

There are many other ways people pray.

It is possible to talk with your God, to lay before her the issues that trouble or excite, and to put into words your view of the world. Apart from whatever conversation might ensue, such praying will help you be clear as you can what you feel, and why you feel it.

To love God in this way means to confide as to your utterly best and most trusted friend. You seek to be truthful to one who knows you utterly, who knew you before you were born and will know you when you have left the earth.

When I seek my own truth while praying, I feel it in my body. Feet, gut, solar plexus: they know in ways my mind, narrowly interpreted, doesn't.

To pray in any authentic manner, we must be willing actually to do something. Prayer won't just happen of its own accord.

To love God with your whole strength means to enable "business with God" to take place, not just when it suits you or when you feel the need.

And "whole" means what it says. People sometimes talk about their "spiritual side": as though spirituality was a pastime like embroidery or building model railways. But everything is spiritual, everything we do or say or think...

the concept is worse than useless if it refers only to a range of pious or niche activities.

To love God with your whole strength means to love God with everything that makes you you. Everything. I used to walk about wearing the dark clothes and white collar of a priest. Therein lay a temptation: to inhabit a cherished ecclesiastical fantasy-world, not unattractive in its way, and imagine that by so doing I was helping others draw nearer to God. Fortunately I had a mentor in Martin Israel who was scathing about the deceptiveness of supposedly spiritual glamour of any kind.

And family life reinforced the message. Our partners and children are unlikely to be taken in by what we dress up as. They see us as we are.

And what are we? In the first place, bodies, of such complexity and energy we might almost consider ourselves separate worlds, planets.

The first thing to do, in order to love God with your whole strength, is: love that strength, that power of nature that is your own unique, extraordinary body. It is the gift of Gaian life here below, carrying genetic traces of thousands of people who have preceded you on this earth and who constitute your lineage. It is your sacred identity right now.

Potentially that identity includes organs of sight and hearing, touch and taste, evolved over millennia. It includes, again potentially, ability not only to think but to enact, moving with lower limbs and grasping and manipulating with upper. The central nervous system, for each of us, is the axis mundi, pillar of the world.

And then there are those profound and subtle eco-systems of sex: carriers of life itself and of so much delight and longing and sorrow.

In amongst all of that is a feature known as "hara"

(in martial arts), or sometimes "bottom": your and my potential groundedness in our lower abdomen. If we can relax into hara, we can attain a bodily sense of belonging and connectedness with earth and all its creatures. "Good bottom" writes William Bloom "supports us in staying calm and watchful, when otherwise we might be wobbling from overstimulation and anxiety."[73]

Hara might be engaged through simple exercises such as the Inner Smile, where you imagine a sunbeam of love from your mind and heart warming down into bowels and gut. Our digestive subways are warrens of stupendous complexity: their nervous systems are said to constitute a second brain, independent of the first but operating, if we are healthy, in concert with it.

To love with your whole strength, you need to notice and not take for granted (let alone disparage) your original strength, your body.

If I consider my body, as St Paul famously or notoriously wrote, a "temple of the Holy Spirit" (1 Corinthians 6:19), then I will be observant, careful what I use it for. I say notoriously, because that line of Paul's used to be drummed into us Catholic children as part of an obsessive vigilance against any sexual arousal or freedom. Unfortunately that had the effect of turning "God" into perpetually outraged tyrant, stultifying not so much sexual longings as spiritual ones.

Clearly to love with your whole strength, or just live a tolerable life for that matter, involves discipline, boundaries. Geburah, severity, "you shall not," is part (not whole) of

---

73 William Bloom, The Power of Modern Spirituality, Piatkus, 2011, p.80

the divine image in us. I've described above how, hearing the sorrows of model Georgie long ago at art school, I began to understand how Christian prohibitions round sex were meant to shield people. Those prohibitions, however, were often rooted neither in love nor in knowledge but in fear. Hence, rather than protect people, they ran a risk of infantilizing them, while diverting sexuality into quicksands of obsession and neurosis, with miserable and at times ghastly results.

Anything we do for the good is going to involve acts of will: boundaries...curating what we watch and listen to... unfollowing egregores...awareness of consequences of our actions for self and others.

To try to live a tolerably decent life: it's an ongoing voyage, isn't it? Doubtless there will be catastrophes and crazy episodes along the way: that's how we learn, if we do.

Also mayday calls. None of us goes it alone. We're reliant on one another. We must be willing to trust, and capable of being trusted.

To love God with your whole strength is not to imagine you have a "spiritual" side and then various other unrelated sides. What could be more spiritual than making love to someone? What could be more pertinent to soul than how I handle money?

Loving God with my whole strength is about appreciating the power given me and taking care how I use it: to heal and not to maim...to build and not to undermine...to enhance and not to degrade.

But like most other humans, I have failed in that. Continuously.

So I express sorrow. Being Christian, I make my prayer

through Jesus Christ, whose cross is the very icon of our human capacity to screw up, and who supposedly said "Father, forgive them; for they do not know what they are doing" (Luke 23:34).

As a young adult, I used to pray as far as possible kneeling unsupported, arms spread out. It was a posture that seemed properly disciplined, a cold bath of awe, and for awhile it worked for me, clearing away mental obstacles and enabling me to focus.

Much has been written by people of all traditions about bodily posture in meditation and prayer. What everyone agrees is that we bring our bodies to whatever it is we do: spiritual practice is not purely a mental act. It involves the whole of us.

I am past an age now where kneeling unsupported would help: it would be distractingly painful. So I sit, as unsupported and upright as possible. I am admiring of those who can manage oriental seating postures; but that, again, would not assist me, even were it physically doable. The aim, always, is relaxed concentration, so I can be fully present to whatever prayer takes place.

You, the reader, may be adept at yoga, or at tai chi or some other bodily form of meditation. May your practice flourish, and go from strength to strength! Or maybe you meditate through walking, or cycling or swimming or surfing or in some other physical way. Discover your dharma! Find out what it is that unlocks your heart and reveals your soul and retunes your mind!

And then, make sure to do it.

In the Christian ecclesiastical environments in which I have whiled away much time, the commonest traditional manner of worshipping God with your whole strength is through ritual. Most churches, even the plainest and most Protestant, use ritual one way or another.

I was once invited to preach (unlikely though it might seem) to a traditionally-minded Presbyterian congregation noted for their non-liturgical sobriety. At the start of their worship, the oldest man present shuffled the length of the church carrying an enormous black Bible which he managed to deposit, as though with his dying gasp, onto a lectern at the front. It was a most dramatic opening ritual (considering they were a congregation who explicitly rejected ritual), expressing, as nothing else could, those men and women's costly commitment to the Word of God.

Ritual opens a space within the everyday where what is sacred (or magical, or different) can be experienced, made manifest. Every human tradition or religion has done ritual some way or other. We know not all communication is in words...music, for instance, is pre-verbal in its subtlety and expressiveness. Creatures such as bats or dolphins feel their way through the world by sonar, trees are allegedly in silent communication with one another; and we humans disclose meaning in a variety of ways using our bodies. We do it all the time in everyday life; dance and mime may take us further (not me, admittedly. I am to dance what a cat is to bel canto).

Meaning that can't be explained verbally doesn't necessarily lack eloquence. The divine worshipped bodily is one whose Logos may be encountered throughout the cosmos myriads of ways; not merely in what we humans consider words.

There are still many Christians, myself included, who were taught the sign of the cross at an early age.

The sign of the cross is a momentary ritual in which you touch, first your forehead, then the centre of your chest, then (in the version I was taught) your left and right shoulders: "in the name of the Father and of the Son and of the Holy Spirit." I have done that simple action daily since I was little. Anyone can do it; thereby, the theory is, you fortify yourself with blessing. That's certainly how it's always felt to me.

Yet "The reason for doing this" wrote a certain scholar, about the sign of the cross, "...is to awaken and activate these Centres" (i.e. head, heart and shoulder), "...to correlate and distribute their various energies, and to suffuse, via the activity of these Centres...(the) whole Sphere of Sensation with...Light and Fire..."[74] Those words, surprising to me, are perhaps a reminder that ritual practices are often rooted in an understanding of our bodies as not merely physical, but subtle.

"The Identity of the Sacred, the Generative Mystery" writes American mystic David Spangler "manifests the original subtle energy which gives rise to all creation. In mystical and spiritual traditions, this primal energy is simply called 'Light.' We are embedded in, surrounded by, filled with, and created from this Light, as is every other thing from star to atom."[75]

You will know, probably better than I do, that such subtle awareness is vitally important in many forms of non-invasive healing. "The Human Energy Field" wrote Barbara Ann Brennan "...can be described as a luminous body that surrounds and interpenetrates the physical body,

---

74 Peter Roche de Coppens, The Nature and Use of Ritual, Llewellyn, 1985, p.85

75 David Spangler, Working with Subtle Energies, Lorian, 2016, pp.11,12

emits its own characteristic radiation and is usually called the 'aura'."[76]

It seems possible even for earthbound individuals to observe this so-called aura; I have sometimes done so myself.

Various working models of our "subtle" being may easily be found. Considering they are pictures of dynamic systems, and bearing in mind the complexity even of our physical bodies, it's no surprise these don't necessarily agree in every detail.

Barbara Ann Brennan again: "There is a vertical flow of energy that pulsates up and down the field in the spinal cord. It extends out beyond the physical body above the head and below the coccyx. I call this the main vertical power current. There are swirling cone-shaped vortexes called chakras in the field. Their tips point into the main vertical power current..."[77] That gives you a flavour.

As is well-known, the (oriental) system described above identifies seven chakras. Western practices grounded in Kabbalah attune to subtle vibrations in different, though complementary, ways.

Openness to non-material reality pertains, not only to strength but to heart, soul and mind. To love God with our whole strength entails connection with presence at every level: visible and invisible, gross and subtle.

Jesus seems (to me) to have said: don't content yourself merely with old words.

---

76 Barbara Ann Brennan, Hands of Light, Bantam, 1988, p.41
77 Ibid. p.43

His "first commandment" is to engage the living presence, now, with heart, soul, mind, strength. Not just to read about it, really to do it.

He considered that the first part of the key to life.

SIXTEEN

The second is this

When Jesus was asked by the scribe "Which commandment is the first of all?" his answer was clear and straightforward. "Love the Lord your God." But he then immediately added a second, indivisible from the first: love your neighbour as yourself.

It's entirely possible to imagine a scenario where the scribe asked the question and Jesus replied, "You are to obey the righteous laws of God, and judge others accordingly".

But Jesus didn't say that.

Now, the little catch-all word "Love" needs, as we preachers like to put it, unpacking; and then again, whatever path we practise has to include justice somehow or other... doesn't it?

What people of my time and place have come to assume, however, is neither love nor justice, but cosmic indifference.

Look out at the unimaginable vastness any night sky spreads before us. Imagine the chasms of geological time. See around us, in people we know, random illnesses, accidents, untimely deaths.

Can any of that seriously speak of love or justice? Surely we humans are no more than an accidental pox on the surface of a tiny planet soon to be obliterated amid the changes and chances of a transient galaxy?

"My God, my God, why have you forsaken me?" That has been a familiar cry down the centuries. In the words of Psalm 22 uttered by Jesus on the cross, it is of course still within a relationship, however anguished.

But even abandonment can seem an illusion. There may be no-one abandoning us.

Not long ago a remedy for such despair might have been exhortation to faith in one or other of the traditional representations of deity.

The two "Great Commandments" of Jesus have been foundation stones of my life; therefore I am hardly about to disregard trodden religious paths. But I know faith based only on clan loyalty is unlikely to be able withstand whatever fires may come.

So what does the Jesus of the gospels have to say to us, in response to existential nihilism?

He seems not to say, or at least not straight away, go back to the scriptures, obey the righteous laws, believe the authorized doctrines, join the One True community of the Rightly Guided.

What he does say, first and foremost, is (you have heard it several times now): Love. Not faith, important though that undoubtedly is.

Faith and practice are seen as following on from love, not the other way round.

I've just written about openness of heart, soul, mind and strength toward the originating mystery we may call God or something else. ("It's like trying to have a conversation" a woman once told me "with someone very shy." I remember replying that the lover, though shy, seemed nothing if not persistent).

People of my generation who adopt an atheistic stance have tended to be sneery about faith, presuming it a throwback to a past age, an obsolete mental crutch. Objectivity and science are here to cure us of all that primitive nonsense.

But what Jesus describes first and foremost, as the answer to our alienation, is not faith at all, but love.

Sciences, hard-won human traditions, prime us for wonder and knowhow. One of the reasons I'm grateful to have lived in my own time has been the brilliance of astronomy; another, the excellence of dentists.

Were I planning a love affair, however, I probably wouldn't start with a spreadsheet. Science, no matter how ingenious, is unlikely to see a path to originating mystery (and probably must remain agnostic to do its job).

And that's because ultimate light is not another thing, observable through telescopes like a supernova. It may (or presumably may not?) become apparent to you...if it does, that may be in some style utterly different from what I've written about.

Presence is how I named it earlier; that's just my word; the presence is partly mine as well as its. We are in territory here, not of objectivity but of resonance, relationship, entanglement.

And that's the kind of knowing...not knowing about but resonating with...that Jesus seems to be commending as our best approach to the vast, seemingly indifferent cosmos with its myriad dimensions and creatures. "The second is like, namely this: Love your neighbour as yourself."

The love Jesus points to will have within it willingness to engage and, all-importantly, empathize. Judgements will have their part, but further down the line. Empathy first.

However: what I witness in my immediate surroundings, as well as in my head, is often a determination to categorize and interpret and judge, well before any listening has even been attempted, let alone connection made.

"By love" wrote the unknown fourteenth-century author of the Cloud of Unknowing "may He be getyn and holden; bot bi thought neither." The medieval author was writing about our relationship with God; but the same is surely true of the connections we make with other people and with life itself. Objective knowledge can open the treasures of the cosmos. But unless our objectivity is also undergirded and warmed by empathy, it is likely to remain the incomprehensible language of an alien universe.

Within the Christian thought-world where I have spent my life, the usual representation of divine love involves a cross in some shape or form. There is a radiate cross over my desk as I write, Celtic in style. At its centre is a star-shaped symbol of infinity: the four segments each have Trinitarian motifs of presence within them; and round the periphery is a halo decorated with patterns of swirling life-entanglement.

Such a cross is a reminder of the collision and intersection of heavenly and earthly. Each of us may be imagined as a point of intersection. The vertical is our to-ing and fro-ing with spirit, our "business with God". The horizontal has to do with the second commandment, "which is like, namely this: Love your neighbour as yourself." Both are pictured as one single energy.

The use of the cross symbol predated Jesus Christ. But then came his death and the events following; and from that point on, the cross has been laden with mystery and complexity and power. An obscene gibbet of random terror turned into a totem of existential hope.

Christ's self-offering may seem to portray something about creation itself. His arms spread out and nailed to wood have been understood as covenant, forgiveness, blessing, embrace...in which the whole earth is invited to share.

It is to that vital embrace that the remainder of this book now turns.

Within the antique Christian traditions of Orthodoxy and Catholicism, the cross is sometimes portrayed with two or three horizontal bars: a long one in the middle, and shorter ones top or bottom. Traditional faith gives to these higher or lower beams profound meanings, which I am not qualified to expound.

What I am qualified to do, however, is attempt to discuss the second commandment of Jesus.

I am going to start by dividing love of neighbour into three parts, illustrated by three bars on an imaginary cross. The long central horizontal bar will relate to our fellow humans. The short beam at the bottom can represent material creation, mineral, vegetable and animal worlds. The short beam at the top can suggest invisible realms and their supposed inhabitants.

All creatures are our neighbours. We are instructed to love them, "as yourself."

In what follows I hope to ask, *a*: what that's supposed to mean? *b*: how we might do it? and *c*: what difference might any of that make?

SEVENTEEN

Love your neighbour (i)

"Our fidelity to and love of Christ" wrote the inter-religious scholar Raimon Pannikar "do not alienate us from our kindred-which includes angels, animals, plants, the earth, and, of course, men and women."[78] It is exactly in that spirit that I will be moseying round Jesus' great, vital and hugely challenging commandment to love our neighbour. As outlined above, to help with it I am picturing a cross with three horizontal beams. The smaller one at the bottom, a footrest as it were, represents the material world in all its magnificence, non-human. What does it mean for us to love our non-human fellow-inhabitants of earth?

Gaia as I first encountered her was outer London in the aftermath of the terrible Second World War.

My original home was by a main road busy with cars and red buses. Nearby, as mentioned above, were "bomb sites", remains of houses with their insides exposed. As we lived not far from London's then only airport, propeller-driven airliners would pass low overhead. A thrilling place to be taken was the "iron bridge": here I could observe express trains approaching, pistons pummelling, and then whooshing underneath in clouds of pungent steam.

The house where we lived faced what had once been

---

78 Raimon Panikkar, trs. Alfred DiLascia, Christophany, Orbis, 2004, p.168

a village green. On the other side of that green was a path; and among my earliest memories are toddling walks with Mum down that long, long track. The ditches were piled with old bed frames and other rubbish; the surroundings seemed, even to my childish eye, shattered and scabby.

But the path led eventually, through a gateway, into another world: the magically preserved environs of what had formerly been a gentleman's estate. Here suddenly were open fields, fine trees: oak, elm, cedars of Lebanon. Here was a lake, with noisy congregations of wild birds. Nature was calmly on display, protected somehow from the twentieth century's travails.

"Matter" is one letter from the Latin "Mater," mother. I was taught as a child that God was our (somewhat distant) father, looking down from on high. I don't remember anyone telling me earth was our mother. On the other hand, being Catholics, we paid great attention to Mary, mother of Jesus. Mary is one letter from the Latin "Mare", sea. Though we lived far inland, sea was a powerful feature in our lives, because my grandparents owned a small house on the channel coast; they had bought it for next to nothing at the beginning of the war, when everyone feared an invasion. We used to have it for school holidays. So growing up, there was a sort-of second home, practically on the beach. I could view the sea from my bed, and hear gulls calling all hours of the day and night.

What could be more beguiling than rock pools, and the tiny creatures that scuttle and swim about in their miniature worlds, until the next tide washes in? What could be more sensuous (I thought as a five year old) than sea weed? What could be more awesome, more liberating, than the vast wild ocean itself? I longed to be there, was impatient for the next visit. I think love for our "sea mother" is, to start with, visceral. Mine was, anyway.

Presence? Maybe...though of a different, thrilling sort to any encountered in religious devotion. On the beach I felt more alive than anywhere else, and it was (and is) a whole-body aliveness, tingling up through my feet and baptizing my entire being.

That wonder has remained, and not only by the sea. Like many older people I now help nurture a small garden, playing my small part in the magic of growth, as everything reaches for the sun. The "earth mother" enthrals, as still does the "sea mother".

"The earth is the Lord's" wrote the psalmist "and all that is in it, the world, and those who live in it; for he has founded it on the seas and established it on the rivers." (Psalm 24: 1, 2)

Orthodox religion was quick to claim nature for its own. At school and in church we Catholic children were taught the Biblical stories of the seven days of creation and that business with Adam and Eve and the talking snake; and they were understood literally, as reports of events that had happened at the beginning of time, exactly as described.

However, one of the nuns who taught at our school, a sweet young woman tightly enclosed in her starched linen and black cloth habit, out of which she smiled and giggled, maintained a "nature table." On it were dead leaves and nuts and bits of tree, a bird's nest and a few broken eggs... and, in the middle of it all: a fossil.

We used occasionally to find fossils on the beach. We were told they were remains of animals that had lived long before there were humans. That did, of course, contradict the straightforward Bible narrative.

I tried to imagine the loneliness of distant ages on

that familiar shore. Meanwhile, on my grandparents' bookshelves was one volume in particular that seized me and wouldn't let go. It was entitled "Extinct Monsters, and Creatures of Other Days,"[79] and inside were scary drawings of such beasts as Triceratops and Tyrannosaurus Rex.

One day, I noticed that each of the millions of pebbles rolled by the tide was gloriously different from all the others. "They'd have some stories to tell" Mum said. I tried to imagine what those stories might be. I sank my fingers in cold shingle and felt the skin-caress of sand and seawater.

We may read about prehistoric animals or clashes of galaxies long ago. We can try to conjure up oceans of superheated plasma, or the titanic emptiness of interstellar space. Not many of us domesticated humans can really begin to fathom any of it. Yes, you or I might peer through a telescope at light reaching us across aeons from some remote nebula.

But if I hold a beach-pebble in my hand, though I still don't comprehend the mystery, I can at least make some sort of a skin-connection.

"Whoever does not love does not know God, for God is love." (1 John 4: 8) That sentence seems the epicentre of Christian faith, a path I have tried (though often failed) to walk. But what might be described as the love of God in creation is (except in self-giving) barely parallel to anything we could begin to imagine, let alone emulate.

What does it mean to speak of divine "love" in connection with, say, stars forming in Cone Nebula, or galactic collisions in Perseus, or even the century-old storm on our neighbouring planet Jupiter, clearly visible from earth?

---

79 By the Revd H.N.Hutchinson, originally published in 1892.

Perhaps you or I just shrug our shoulders and answer: freedom?

Indeed... but with it, something else, of unimaginable otherness: stupendous, titanic originating energy. What name might we give such force, such power?

We might (lamely) label it Eros...for want of any other word.

It's that force, or Eros, that gives life to you and me: but filtered and mediated through countless veils and levels and dilutions, so as to render it bearable. If we were to witness what I have been calling presence in anything remotely resembling "neat" form, we would instantly be combusted.

Presence, in my own narrow experience, can often be accessed remotely through prayer, silent or otherwise. It might touch us in nature or through music. You could even glimpse a tincture of presence in something as random as the surprise of a lover's smile... and so on, diluted to the nth degree, down infinite levels...

The point I'm labouring is that originating mystery can't be (to us) just some isolated magical thing, confronting us from a specific magic place, separate from all the other places. We can't beam in on divine Ground Zero.

Nuns taught me long ago that God is everywhere, and contains everything.

But I also learnt that everything, thus contained, is free to go its mysterious way: galaxies collide, dinosaurs roam; sometimes things are "all fuckin' shit" and the only prayer becomes "My God, my God, why have you forsaken me?"

Yet through all that apparent chaos, here we are, contained by an originating force, an originating gravity.

We may glimpse it in what I call presence: something we are capable of knowing, within and among us.[80]

There is (to me) a felt sweetness in that: hence my own certainty love is in it: the "Love that moves the sun and the other stars."

So, whether or not we consciously recognise divine presence, if we give ourselves single-heartedly in love maybe we can parallel, microcosmically, that energy that gave birth to the universe.

And through such love we might be privileged, in our own tiny but not unimportant way, to become co-creators.

OK, I know people have dreamt or fantasised about the "Kingdom of Heaven" and imagined they could bring it in through human power or political coercion. And I am only too well aware of the crack through everything, "original sin", the shadow. I see and lament it every day in my own words and actions.

Which brings me back to what it might mean to love my non-human neighbours.

In the famous story at the beginning of Genesis, God is pictured inventing all the various living creatures: "And it was so. God made the wild animals of the earth of every kind, and everything that creeps upon the ground of every kind. And God saw that it was good. Then God said, 'Let us make humankind in our image, according to our likeness; and let them have dominion over the fish of the sea, and over the birds of the air, and over the cattle, and over all the wild animals of the earth, and over every creeping thing that creeps upon the earth.'" (Genesis 1: 25, 26)

---

80 (See Luke 17:21).

Those words have been argued over for millennia, none more than the dread word "dominion." It describes the power we humans continue to wield, so much that our age is now referred to as the Anthropocene.

But oh, the ruin our dominion has entailed. We haven't, to put it mildly, got very far learning how to co-create.

I expect we all remember moments when that dawned on us.

I have a memory from when I was about twelve of visiting the old walled park near where we used to live. It had been a place apart from the ravaged landscape round about. We had moved, I hadn't been there for a while: and in the meantime a motorway had been ploughed across it. I remember looking down from a footbridge at the concrete road and the tin cars hurtling beneath and noticing almost for the first time the imperious crushing ugliness of my own world.

Of course, the park was itself an artificial human construct. But it had seemed, to my childish eyes, in harmony with nature. Now that harmony was no more.

You will be well aware that the great challenge of my lifetime and probably yours is the despoliation of earth, Gaia, our mother, through reckless exploitation by us humans. Climate change affected by our doings since the industrial revolution is one whole aspect, and another is the crushing and annihilation of wild nature. You will not need to be told any of that. You are living with the consequences.

We live in an artificial environment, fashioned out of the stuff of nature, usually with little regard for the non-human, not so much loving our neighbours as exploiting them to fulfil our wants. Such exploitation goes back to the dawn of humanity but has become far more extreme in my time.

Though we humans have usually behaved cruelly in our dealings with our creaturely neighbours, it became conventional in my lifetime, to blame Christianity especially for this. The little word "dominion" in the Bible passage quoted above was produced in evidence. According to the prosecution, "nature religion that encouraged a holistic, ecocentric attitude of respect for the natural world was replaced by a form of religion that desacralized nature...Disenchanted, nature became little more than raw material."[81]

There is surely some truth in the accusation. It was made by a historian of science called Lynn White back in the 1960s. "In Antiquity every tree, every spring, every hill had its own genius loci, its guardian spirit...Before one cut a tree, or mined a mountain, or dammed a brook, it was important to placate the spirit in charge of that particular situation, and to keep it placated...Christianity made it possible to exploit nature in a mood of indifference to the feelings of natural objects...For nearly two millennia Christian missionaries have been chopping down sacred groves, which are idolatrous because they assume spirit in nature."[82]

Since White's time[83] many have criticised his thesis as flawed and naive.[84] However, it hit a spot, and has

---

81 Christopher Partridge, The Re-Enchantment of the West, Volume 2, T&T Clark 2005, p.51

82 Quoted ibid. p.51. The original article, Lynn White Jr., The Historical Roots of Our Ecological Crisis, is in Science, 10 March 1967, Vol. 155, Issue 3767, pp.1203–1207

83 (It might be worth noting that White was himself an observant Presbyterian Christian).

84 E.g. Bernard Anderson, From Creation to New Creation, Fortress Press, 1994. Ian Bradley, God is Green, Darton, Longman and Todd, 1990. Alister McGrath, The Re-Enchantment of Nature, Doubleday, 2002

continued to do so. Let us presume for a moment what he wrote is true.

When we learn to see through a particular lens, it can change everything. Suppose a woman relocates to a new country. Gradually she absorbs the land's language and customs, and after time has passed the language and customs become her own.

One day she revisits her original homeland. She sees once-familiar sights through what feel like different eyes. Yet those eyes remain the same ones she had before. Her original roots and reflexes are still part of her: overlaid by other experience they may be, but they are still there, even if now understood differently.

During tens of thousands of years, we humans lived in an original homeland. Life there involved an instinctual relationship with earth and sea that would come to be considered primitive. There are still, as I write, tribesmen and women who follow closely the ways of their ancestors, but they are few now, their way of life beleaguered.

"For us" says spiritual teacher and academic Malidoma Some, who was born into the Dagara people of Burkino Faso, "the supernatural is part of our everyday lives. To a Dagara man or woman, the material is just the spiritual taking on form."[85] He quotes a tribal elder: "The centre is both within and without. It is everywhere. But we must realize it exists, find it, and be with it, for without the centre we cannot tell who we are, where we come from, and where we are going...No-one's centre is like someone else's. Find your own centre, not the centre of your neighbour, not the

---

85 Malidoma Patrice Some, Of Water and the Spirit, Penguin, 1994, p.8

centre of your father or mother or family or ancestor but that centre which is yours and yours alone."[86]

But, Malidoma Some continues, "...the indigenous world is not a place where everything flows in harmony, but one in which people must be constantly on the alert to detect and to correct imbalances and illnesses in both communal and individual life."[87]

So naturally we learnt to exploit, to work with but also against the lives and presences with which we shared our planet. On a shelf near where I am writing I keep a little pile of flint tools, chipped out thousands of years ago...I handle them occasionally to remind me of the travails of that vast human family of which I am a member.

In time our search for food, warmth, shelter and medicine became more, power to cultivate, to herd, to invent. Through many millennia we learnt "dominion", and we co-created a world largely artifactual, which is that in which I, and presumably you, have lived our lives. Not the kingdom of heaven. Our big, real, noisy, gritty, competitive everyday.

Now through "dominion", the lights are on at least in one tiny corner of the cosmos; and, unarguably, that was a possibility and a potential...from the remotest microsecond of the most distant Big Bang.

But in order for such potential to be realised, we had to evolve out of the jungle. We had to leave home. So we stopped communing as a matter of course with our earth mother. We began using satellite navigation to plot our journeys.

---

86 Ibid., pp. 198–199
87 Ibid., p.62

Yet, like the woman in a new country[88]we still remain members of our original tribe. Just as she can remind herself of the songs and dialect of her early home, so we too are capable of attuning to the nature, and the spirits, that still surround us and are part of us.

Some of my sophisticated urban contemporaries, for instance, develop what feels to them two-way communication with trees. I've experienced such apparent connection myself: it tunes us to unexpected wavelengths.

(But what do you feel about my mentioning that here? In the time and place I am writing, there is an assumed and mocking taboo round any hint of subtle awareness.)

However any of that may be, "dominion" exercised by humans over our mineral, vegetable and animal neighbours carries with it grave responsibilities. And as we all know, those have, to put it mildly, been neglected.

Lynn White was correct to draw attention to the way his fellow Christians, in particular, had behaved. For what do we find buried amid the teachings of Jesus but this:

"You know that among the Gentiles those whom they recognize as their rulers lord it over them and their great ones are tyrants over them. But it is not so among you; but whoever wishes to become great among you must be your servant, and whoever wishes to be first among you must be slave of all." (Mark 10:42–44)

That, for Christians, is what "dominion" should have meant all along: not tyranny but service. Jesus was of course referring to human relationships first and foremost (though in that too Christians have hardly led by example),

---

88 (and like Malidoma Some, who at the time of writing teaches in America.)

but the words are equally powerful when applied to our other neighbours here in planet earth.

Our relationship with non-human creatures is, to put it mildly, complicated. Both they and we have to eat. Hunting is part of the shadow cast by our material universe. Jesus' early male disciples were fishermen; therefore he must have understood the necessity of predation here on earth.

Even the toughest fisherman, however, has to respect the creatures on which his own life depends. He can't presume automatic harvests. He has to hunt in a way that lets the fish thrive and doesn't destroy that on which they in turn feed.

In our original homeland, we humans allegedly enjoyed reciprocal relationships with the plants and creatures and the whole created universe. Those links didn't rule out killing, but there was supposedly a sense in which various levels of life communicated with one another.

That still seems present, not far beneath the surface. It gets expressed, in my English environment, through deep connections people make with pet animals and with birds, wildlife and trees in their gardens. Sometimes it feels as though it's an original language.

In my lifetime and yours, that original language got overlaid not just with science and materialism but with the vast contraption that is Western production and consumption, the system in which we're enmeshed and from which no apostasy is permitted. Short-term, that delivered us our toys and sweets and fed our addictions. Long-term, it poisoned the air, filled the seas with plastic.

But the science and sophistication we've learnt in our adopted home has also given us eyes to see and power to communicate the harm we have been doing. Might primeval love, freshly awakened and empowered with tech magic, yet begin to cure us of our vandalism?

Ravaged nature, meanwhile, has been delivering our careless human world the first in what might turn out to be a series of shocks. While I have been writing these words, a coronavirus pandemic has stopped our mighty human juggernaut in its tracks worldwide.

Such viruses, as doubtless you know, can jump from animals to humans. Accusing fingers in this case pointed straight away to a particular live animal market.

Here is a description, by naturalist Chris Packham, of scenes from that market viewed on his laptop:

"The footage is blurry, but there are mounds of giant bats baked onto sticks, huge beautifully patterned pythons lying tangled coils on tiled tables, tiny monkeys cowering in cramped cages and, through the bustling crowd of shoppers, you can see dirty crates overflowing with writhing piles of eels, crayfish, ducklings and kittens, all desperately clamouring to escape. The phone camera then pans onto piles of cooked rats or squirrels, rows of tortoises, terrapins, all lined up on a floor awash with blood, and finally, those strangely scaled bodies of pangolins, the most trafficked wild animal on Earth."[89]

Is that not a description of a scene from hell? And yet comparable misery has been witnessed throughout human history, and in all the cities of the world. Primitive religion, too, often amounted to a sacrificial bloodbath.[90] (How might our animal neighbours ever forgive us, in any

---

89 Chris Packham, Megan McCubbin, Back to Nature, Two Roads, 2020, p.39

90 (e.g.1 Kings 8:63)

imagined paying out of justice, for how we have treated them?)

So what might love of our non-human neighbour look like? What can we do about it?

Responses will be as various as people. But I would like especially to mention wonder as a human quality. Wonder, in both senses, ought to be included by Christians as a fourth "theological virtue", along with the traditional ones, faith hope and love.

It may be the wonder we experience when we first encounter some small animal, a newt or baby bird or stag beetle, or even our own pet kitten or puppy, that leads to wondering about the lives of such creatures and then wondering how best to protect them. That was how it was for me, anyway. Our hearts are engaged, and then our minds kick in.

A handicap of some ecological preaching seems to me that it is still chiefly about us, about what will happen to us humans if global warming melts the ice-caps or bees go extinct. Clearly such matters are of profound and immediate urgency. But real love gives, first and foremost. It's not supposed to be primarily self-serving.

I grew up surrounded by the big real noisy gritty world of lorries and buses and aeroplanes and trains, and later of computers and mobile phones. With that goes a "...Story of the Self that economics and genetics have offered, asserting that people are fundamentally motivated by self-interest." Charles Eisenstein: "That way of thinking immerses us. Why are the birds singing? To mark territory and attract a mate. Why are the kittens playing? To practice hunting skills. Why are raspberries so delicious? To invite animals to eat them and poop out the seeds."

He says, "I find these answers dispiriting...All beings yearn toward the exuberant expression of their life force... Let us, then, invite each other into that inherent love for life that lies buried, however deeply, beneath the habits and beliefs of Separation."[91]

Eisenstein speaks of love pragmatic nihilists of my generation were supposed to have forfeited. And yet, when coronavirus came for us and life as we knew it shut down, what did everyone do? We all went outside and marvelled at nature, even though it was wild nature that had bitten back. We discovered all over again our love, for birds and animals and for everything that reaches for the sun. And it became an absolute commonplace for people to say nature had saved them, that without the scream of skylarks or the serenity of trees or the silent beauty of flowers they could not have gone on.

So it seems a very thin plastic film of materialism and consumerism masks our aboriginal souls.

Beneath that film, no matter how dependent on science, we are still children of the wondrous old country: which now cries for rescue from our dominion.

There are tiny steps we can take as individuals to encourage nature: digging out a pond, for instance, which my wife and I did recently in our little back yard. Such a thing might seem insignificant, though not for the creatures that make their lives there. Thousands of such small acts, besides the joy and fascination they provide, can go a little way to offset the poisonous destruction we humans visit upon other parts of our common home.

Becoming interested in life, too, is part of wonder. If I observe and watch tadpoles or pond-skaters or water-

---

91 Charles Eisenstein, Climate, A New Story, North Atlantic Books, 2018, p.145

boatmen or hoverflies, if I notice their beauty and pay attention to their doings, I may become less likely to trash their habitat. Part of love for these our neighbours is getting to know them, which might even lead, sometimes, to the beginnings of communion. (Everyone who works or plays with animals sees each has a unique character).

The truth is, all beings around us, including those we despise or exterminate or consume, express something of the infinite originating mystery. So what might we learn of that creativity by saying, and meaning, Namaste[92] to each and every one of them?

But we know our little hobbyist enthusiasms are not going to be enough, even multiplied millions of times, to save earth our mother from the destruction wrought upon her. For that, something bigger is needed.

Conversion of life, what the gospel calls metanoia, is wildly necessary, not just individually but on a collective, global level. Love for our fellow-creatures and our mother the earth and our mother the sea may require us to be part of movements, thought-forms, egregores (not all are bad) that empower reformation not just of society but of our reluctant selves.

Who or what can save the creatures, Gaia, us?

Rediscovery of what it means to love our neighbours and to exercise dominion not domination?

One great Christian exemplar is the beloved Francis of Assisi. In the words of Francis' biographer Bonaventure, "When he considered the primordial source of all things, he was filled with even more abundant piety, calling creatures,

---

92 Sanskrit, "The divine in me recognizes the divine in you," if I understand it correctly.

no matter how small, by the name of brother or sister, because he knew they had the same source as himself."[93]

Bonaventure recounts various stories about Francis' connections with beings of Earth,[94] his love for them and the difference that made. Such stories have of course usually been dismissed by my know-it-all generation as pious fables.

But they are more than that. They are manifestos of connection: about not treating animals, birds and climatic phenomena as "it" but engaging with them as "you."

The Francis stories suggest a cosmos in which consciousness isn't merely some accidental by-product limited to human brains, but potential everywhere, albeit often in very simple forms. Such a way of looking ("panpsychism") that supposes potential consciousness (not necessarily similar to our own) scattered and mingled everywhere, rather than confined to human brains, not only makes transformative love like Francis' more possible. It connects with the daily experiences of those many people who communicate in heartfelt ways with birds, animals, trees, plants, rivers, mountains, natural phenomena, even though they themselves are surrounded by plastic consumerism.

If you have the slightest idea what I'm talking about... maybe it's because you have experienced the mysterious portals that sometimes appear and disappear in nature?

Through them, we glimpse, sometimes to our amazement, interiority, connectedness...presence. The universe in its immensity can seem far from indifferent in such moments.

The above presents an open goal to debunkers. "Anthropomorphism" (according to biologist Merlin

---

93 Bonaventure, trs. Ewert Cousins, Paulist Press, 1978, pp.254/255
94 See ibid.pp. 254–261

Sheldrake) is orthodoxly considered "...an illusion that arises like a blister in soft human minds."

There are good reasons for such an anathema, Sheldrake says: "...when we humanise the world, we may prevent ourselves from understanding the lives of other organisms on their own terms." "But" he concludes "are there things this stance might lead us to pass over – or forget to notice?"[95]

"Who shall ascend the hill of the Lord?" continues the psalm I quoted earlier "and who shall stand in his holy place? Those who have clean hands and pure hearts..." (Psalm 24 3,4a)

Perhaps our present human level of awareness, far from having peaked, is still only in its foothills. Maybe we have a way to go before we ourselves (never mind other creatures) can begin to claim to be conscious.

Meanwhile it would be good for each of us to find new and intelligent ways, not to exploit or pillage but to understand and cherish the non-human world...maybe even with clean-ish hands and pure-ish hearts: to say, and mean, Namaste to mother earth and mother sea and all their creatures.

---

95 Merlin Sheldrake, Entangled Life, Bodley Head, 2020, p.45

EIGHTEEN

Love your neighbour (ii)

Preachers I have heard on Jesus' "Great Commandments" have often skipped the first one, about loving God, and focussed all their attention on the second. We humans tend to be preoccupied with ourselves!

Jesus tackles the subject of ourselves in an uncompromising way. He tells us we must learn to love. In particular we must learn to love other humans with whom we share our planet...whether we like them or not...

We might need a bit of help with that. We are catastrophically bad at it.

But in any case...how can you or I be commanded to love? Are we not created in such a way that we love some, put up with others and despise a few?

Any Christian preacher with a first-year certificate in Biblical studies will be quick to answer that question by pointing out the differences in various New Testament words done into English as "Love". I won't add to the sermons I and others have given on that ever-popular subject, except to state the obvious: Jesus is not commanding we have intimate or even friendly feelings towards all the people of the world.

What he is telling us to do (in itself a huge, challenging and liberating ask) might also be expressed in the Sanskrit word Namaste mentioned earlier: acknowledge the divine, "I Am," in each and every one. Take each human child seriously, as we hope God does. Protect and cherish their right to be. Help and support our neighbours proactively, like the Samaritan in the story Jesus told to illustrate the teaching.

Understandably there has been some scepticism in my lifetime around supposedly Christian nations' willingness to pay even the slightest attention to any of that.

The twentieth century, in the middle of which I was born, had dawned with high hopes. But as we know, those hopes proved to be mirages.

"World War 1 was fought" (by supposedly Christian combatants) "with the most advanced modern weaponry, and funded with the vast wealth of modern capitalist societies. Machine guns mowed soldiers down in their thousands, while modern medical services kept them alive in waterlogged trenches between battles...World War 2 was both more global and more destructive...With highly mobile armies and massive use of air power, civilian casualties were greater than those of the combatant armies...More than six million people, most of them Jews, died in the industrial slaughter houses of the Holocaust. The war finally ended with the dropping of the world's first atomic weapons... the one dropped on Hiroshima killed 80,000 people almost immediately...A decade later the US and the Soviet Union had developed...even more terrifying weapons that used the power of fusion, the same mechanism that generated power in the heart of the sun."[96]

I grew up in the aftermath of those apocalyptic wars (begun by allegedly Christian nations) with the perpetual

---

96 David Christian, The Anthropocene Epoch, in The Oxford Illustrated History of the World, ed. Felipe Fernandez-Armesto, Oxford University Press, 2019, p.364

threat of something yet more catastrophic always overshadowing us. My grandparents and parents had lived through abysses of human darkness, as had most of the people round us. "Why did God allow it?" I recall Granddad Jack saying one day, shaking his head, after silencing a family party with a horrible recollection from Passchendaele.

I know that when I or any preacher ventures onto the thin ice of love and its evolutionary importance, we are certain to be ridiculed for culpable naivety. What can we hope for, in view of the history of the last hundred years (or any of the thousands of years before)? What responses have we to the towering satanic tsunamis of hatred and fear and lust that seem programmed into our souls?

My first answer might be: at least we are aware of ourselves. We can see who and what we are. We might have some understanding of our instincts and their potential consequences. We have witnessed the "crack through everything."

But second, and for me overwhelmingly more important: the central horizontal bar on the cross, used here to represent our human neighbours, has nailed to it the outstretched arms of Jesus Christ. That agonized gesture portrays as luridly as is possible to imagine the love of the divine for us human children and for all the creatures of earth. It is a naked appalling symbol bloody with meaning. The figure is nailed to the hard wood of the cross, cannot escape the iron nails, is immobilized, cannot break free. There could be no more excruciating image of the utter commitment of the divine to us, literally a covenant signed in blood, with all the sheer impossibility and harshness that entails.

And yet it's given. It has been made real once and for all

in the suffering and death of the man Jesus, who bore the burden of representing God to us. There can be no going back from that. The commitment was made, and cannot be unmade. Therefore, however long it takes, the "Kingdom of God" (so called) will prevail and the satanic forces of greed and destruction will shrivel away and fail. If it were merely down to us humans, I would of course doubt the chances of our human experiment succeeding. But with Christ come to join us, we need have no fear.

(That gives you a sense of what it was like to be on the receiving end of one of my sermons!)

Christian preachers have held forth down the centuries in just such a way about the "saving" death of Christ. I remain convinced as to the huge significance of the event.

Yet...as soon as I introduce such openly religious imagery, I am bringing in something divisive.

Human symbols are felt in legions of ways. What the arms of Christ outstretched on the cross represent for me is original presence reaching out in self-giving love to the whole creation: "Father, forgive them; for they do not know what they are doing" (Luke 23:34).

But the cross has often been wielded with such heavy-handed enthusiasm as to compromise its power as an icon of healing.

The compromise began within scripture itself. In a much-quoted passage of St John's gospel, we read: "For God so loved the world that he gave his only Son, so that everyone who believes in him may not perish but may have eternal life...Those who believe in him are not condemned; but those who do not believe are condemned already, because they have not believed in the name of the only Son of God" (John 3: 16, 18).

There is, needless to say, some subtlety round the Greek word that surfaces in Anglo-Saxon as "believing"; such subtlety is exploited to the full by preachers who long to speak of unconditional divine love.

But nonetheless, even in that most inspired of writings, there appears a simplistic binary, "in/out". Can that really be how presence, origin, God, behaves?

(If so, I am of course "out").

The crack through everything disfigures the very symbol that proclaims restoration.

When I was a child, we were taught that the crucifix (image of the cross specifically with the figure of the dying Jesus attached) represented our Catholic "One True Faith" as contrasted with counterfeit Christianities, Protestant and other. Christ's work was considered to have been for "our" salvation, namely members of that unique exclusive club holding the keys to the Kingdom of Heaven. It was not for anyone else. No-one else had access to it, whatever their deluded preachers might allege. That message was frequently hammered from pulpits, and drummed into us at school.[97]

I had little choice but to live for a while within that universe of fixed beliefs and simplistic explanations, as children do. Sociologist Peter Berger, writing about the infinitely more constrained circumstances of old-time Jews in Western Europe, said that "To be Jewish was a taken-for-granted given of the individual's existence, ongoingly reaffirmed with ringing certainty by everyone in the individual's milieu (including the non-Jews in that milieu)."[98]

We may choose to remain indefinitely in such a world, and we may value and treasure the sense of being part

---

97 (The attitudes expressed towards Protestants and others were, in my particular English environment, mostly pitying, rarely hateful).

98 Peter Berger, The Heretical Imperative, William Collins, 1979, p.29

of "One True" community or tradition, "Rightly Guided." No-one would deny the powerful appeal of such sacred belonging in our dangerous world.

But with the coming of modernity, wrote Berger, "All the individual has to do to get out of his alleged Jewish destiny is to walk out and take the subway. Outside, waiting, is the emporium of life-styles, identities and religious preferences..."[99] That was how it was for me in my Catholic environment, and doubtless for millions of others raised in traditional faith communities.

You may remember the Greek Orthodox bishop who welcomed delegates to an inter-faith conference by declaring that "Truth resides in the Greek Orthodox Church. My humble advice to you all is to join it."[100] Given our world can seem a terrifying place, it's no surprise faith communities often circle the wagons, especially if stories in their scriptures and rituals hark back to golden times when truth was known and virtue practiced. Such "fundamentalist" wagon-circling, even if done gently as by the Greek bishop, seems characteristically human.

When we hear of religious fundamentalists, we might imagine fiery zealots angrily proclaiming their crusade or jihad. Or maybe we picture some exclusive conventicle, stern bearded men and cowed women in headscarves. But in less obvious ways the fundamentalist disposition remains near the heart of what might be called "mainstream" religion.

I spent the middle years of my life working as an Anglican parish priest in suburban and rural England. During my early days the big issue consuming churches I served was whether or not women might be ordained. That question

---

99 Ibid., p.30
100 See chapter nine.

had risen as part of the twentieth century's freeing of the female gender from earlier patriarchal assumptions; and in churches it proved hugely divisive. Those passionately opposed to such ordinations were usually straightforward, loyal church members (female as well as male), who would express terror that blasphemy was about to be perpetrated.

The reasons opponents gave usually had to do with breaking tradition considered to reach back to Jesus and his original followers. I don't recall anyone, in the numerous, interminable and often angry debates I attended, quoting the following Biblical Mitzvah:

"When a woman has a discharge of blood that is her regular discharge from her body, she shall be in her impurity for seven days, and whoever touches her shall be unclean until the evening. Everything upon which she lies during her impurity shall be unclean; everything also upon which she sits shall be unclean...Whoever touches anything upon which she sits shall wash his clothes, and bathe in water, and be unclean until the evening...Thus you shall keep the people of Israel separate from their uncleanness, so that they do not die in their uncleanness by defiling my tabernacle that is in their midst" (Leviticus 15:19–20, 22, 31).

The passion with which an unreasonable and damaging exclusion was argued against seemed to me rooted, not so much in nostalgic traditionalism as in dismay at, and hatred of, human bodies, specifically female ones. This dismay had been passed on, according to psychologist Ann Baring, "...not only in the Semitic cultures of the Near and Middle East, and in Greek and Roman culture, but also further to the East, in cultures such as those of India and China, wherever a powerful controlling male priesthood allied to social custom assigned and enforced a subservient position on women. These ideas...entered mainstream

Christian teaching and were responsible for an enormous amount of suffering for women whose inferior and sexual nature came to be seen as the main impediment standing between man and God. It is as if a spell were cast on the Christian psyche..."[101]

Needless to say, such naked gynophobia rarely surfaced openly in the Anglican arguments, but bubbled up from underground, an unacknowledged blood-red reservoir of ancient fear. Probably few of those involved would have endorsed the old taboos. Their emotion in such an incoherent cause sometimes surprised even them.

Comparable stress, at the time of writing, surrounds the subject of same-sex affinity within Christian and other religious communities. Again, what comes up is more than simple disapproval: rather, fear of defilement, rooted in ancient curses.[102]

Religious fundamentalism as here touched on is more than simply a preference for some practices and a dislike of others. It is the expression of a belief that such and such is absolutely and finally the will of God, to be obeyed to the letter in order that divine wrath might be avoided. Certain perdition awaits all who have not conducted themselves in whatever is decreed the legitimate way, or who belong to the wrong tribe. The "One True" or "Rightly Guided" community is the only place salvation may be found. The proper ceremonies must be carried out by duly authorized ministers according to certain eternally-valid forms. Otherwise, all spiritual striving is in vain.

Ironically if you consider Jesus' maxim "In everything do to others as you would have them do to you" (Matthew

---

101 Ann Baring, The Dream of the Cosmos, Archive, 2013, p.165
102 Such as Leviticus 20:13

7:12) as genuinely fundamental, what this set of reflexes tends to produce is disrespect for the other, often spilling over into hatred.

A further problem, however, if we are attempting to witness to things of God, is that the deity thus obeyed can seem (where do we begin?) petty, mean-minded, cruel, laughable: not so much original presence as a cartoon tinpot tyrant. Are we really supposed to take seriously an immortal being scandalised by menstrual fluids?

That is why I have found religious conservatism (in which I was once a willing player) so often exasperating. When we are content to remain fundamentalist, we cede what is fundamental. Love eludes us.

I have concentrated here on religious fundamentalism in Christian places with which I am familiar, because, rather than opening life to become a spiral into the infinite, it keeps good people shut in windowless rooms where the only stories allowed to be told are ones authorized by a few old men in headdresses. In so doing it encourages a view of people as not only unbeloved but hopelessly deluded and lost.

Consequently, it's still sometimes stated as fact that if there had been no religion there wouldn't ever have been wars. My erstwhile art tutor Jonathan was fond of repeating that platitudinous meme, with an air of long-suffering wisdom; and as a sixteen year old I was briefly impressed.

If only life was that uncomplicated!

Men have always gone to war, on numerous supposed pretexts. Religion has sometimes been a powerful trigger, but so have territorial claims, pre-emptive fears and all sorts of other excuses. Any student of history will be able to reel off causal factors for conflicts ancient and modern.

War is something we humans do.

Jesus would have accepted soldiering as a fact of life in his distempered environment. Roman centurions were not noted for their tenderness or gentility, but Jesus was willing to accept a plea for help from one of them, and commended the man for his faith (Matthew 8: 5–13, Luke 7:2–10).

Like many of my contemporaries, despite having lived through a time of comparative peace (terrorism apart) in my own country, I am a child of war. My grandfather Jack met my grandmother Molly through being wounded in the 1918 Battle of Megiddo and transported to the Cairo hospital where Molly was nursing. War stirred everything up and mixed everything up, as it has done down the centuries.

"Humanity is mad!" wrote a young French soldier in his diary at Verdun in 1916. "It must be mad to do what it is doing. What a massacre. What scenes of horror and carnage! I cannot find words to translate my impressions. Hell cannot be so terrible. Men are mad!"[103] Such madness had always been in the blood of the males of our species: wars, crusades, jihads, border raids have been instigated and fought by young men down the ages. "My heart was full of sorrow, till I thought of the Honour at stake" a Welsh soldier wrote, remembering "chums" slain in the trenches in 1915. "Better death than shame," he concluded.[104] It's hard to imagine a more persuasive

---

103 Second Lieutenant Alfred Joubaire, in Martin Gilbert: The First World War, HarperCollins 1994, p.250

104 Private E. Gordon Hall, 30th November 1915, in an album belonging to my grandmother Molly, who had nursed him.

egregore, among males of our species, than "Honour", especially when it touches the pride and self-respect of tribes or nations.

Nothing I write or you read can do justice to the miseries endured by those caught in the conflicts of the twentieth century. I live in a small terraced house in the east of England. From this house in autumn 1914 a young man went off to serve his country, one among hundreds of thousands. His name was Frank Barton. He endured the trenches' vermin and fear for four years, only to be killed in 1918 a week before the armistice. This very room here where I am sitting, with its wooden floorboards and Victorian fireplace, would have been part of the home Barton remembered down those four dreadful years. The house next door lost three sons. And so on, across Europe, across the world. In the second war, women and children on both sides of the conflict suffered, as you know, the nightmare of aerial bombardment. My contemporaries and I grew up listening to our elders' tales...though some would never tell anything about any of it. There was no shortage of damaged people when I was young.

"It is wonderful with what coolness and indifference" wrote Samuel Johnson in Christian London in 1771 "the greater part of mankind see war commenced. Those that hear of it at a distance, or read of it in books, but have never presented its evils to their minds, consider it as little more than a splendid game."[105] (He went on to describe "... the sudden glories of paymasters and agents, contractors and commissaries...who...laugh from their desks...hoping

---

105 Samuel Johnson, Thoughts on the late Transactions Respecting Falkland's Islands, 1771, in R.W.Chapman, ed., Johnson Prose & Poetry, Oxford, 1922, p. 129

for a new contract from a new armament, and computing the profits...)"[106]

Is it not time we recognised armed conflict for the "extremity of evil"[107] that it is, and strained every sinew to evolve away from it? How can I love my neighbour as myself, while threatening him and his family and his neighbourhood and his whole nation with destruction?

Unfortunately, in Jewish and Christian scriptures, "wrath"[108] was sometimes attributed to God. People then thought that as they waged their human wars of conquest or revenge, they were somehow imitating the divine. To give one of numerous examples, Paul famously wrote that "Much more surely ...now that we have been justified by (Christ's) blood, will we be saved through him from the wrath of God."[109] The word Paul used is associated with divine judgement, that whole department of boundaries and karma imagined in the Kabbalistic "Tree of Life" as a branch called Geburah (directly opposite Chesed, compassion).

In a trivial way, such "wrath" might be what I imitate if pulling up weeds in the garden: necessary destructive action clearing a space for something new to happen. (Even if we're compassionate, we might sometimes long for God to do a little weeding in human affairs).

However, severity and "wrath" are surely God's business, not ours. In the much-loved Indian scripture the Bhagavad Gita, Krishna tells Arjuna that "when a man sees that the God in himself is the same God in all that is, he hurts

---

106 Ibid., p.130
107 Ibid., p.129
108 Several different Hebrew words are rendered in English bibles as "wrath."
109 Romans 5:8,9

not himself by hurting others: then he goes indeed to the highest Path."[110]

But if we are to practice this essential craft, love, rather than simply preach about it, we are going to need help. And for Christians one beloved helper, about whom I have said nothing so far, is the figure referred to by many honorifics and titles but universally known as Mary, that name so close to the Latin word for the sea.

"There is not a shadow of doubt for anyone who takes the spiritual life of mankind seriously, " wrote Valentin Tomberg, "...that the Blessed Virgin Mary is not an ideal only, nor an archetype of the unconscious...but rather a concrete and living individuality-like you or I- who suffers, loves and rejoices. It is not only the children of Fatima, the child Bernadette at Lourdes..., who have witnessed the 'Lady', but also numerous adults across the centuries, including our own. Numerous meetings still remain intimate and undivulged...meetings with the Blessed Virgin are so numerous and so well-attested that one must certainly at least admit their objective reality... One meets the Blessed Virgin inevitably when one attains a certain intensity of spiritual aspiration...This meeting... is as 'natural' for the spiritual domain as the fact of having a mother is natural in the domain of one's terrestrial family."[111]

Tomberg wrote those words as part of his meditation on the Tarot card called Force, or Strength. The image on the card is of a young woman holding open the jaws of a lion, seeming to use neither force nor strength but her own calm authority. The woman is a figure of genial

---

110 Bhagavad Gita 13:28, trs. Juan Mascaro, Penguin, 1962, p.101
111 Meditations on the Tarot, pp.280/281

innocence, able to befriend the lion as Francis did the wolf at Gubbio. This, says Tomberg, is not something strange and extraterrestrial. It is latent within us all. He calls it "...the magic of virgin Nature...truth is revealed through the fusion and not through a clash...Quarrelling will never lead to the truth, as long as one does not give it up and seek for peace...the force which is at work here is that of the Virgin..."[112]

Now I know perfectly well that some of the traditions surrounding Mary have their off-putting features. But, to put it mildly, so do the masculine tribal flag-worshipping, foot-stamping, anthem-singing death-cults with their satanic paraphernalia of weapons. Mary, meanwhile, is the friend of all who seek for peace: and this is either the future of the human race or humanity has no future.

Mary, our sister charged with mothering the "Son of God", shows in so doing the divinity of "I Am" in each human child: something not extraterrestrial and weird but normal. When she came alongside me one evening it wasn't with cosmic fanfares or lights in the sky, but unexpectedly, in an understated friendly way amid routine business.

"She infuses strength into the many who are threatened... She is drawn to those who have experienced travail, challenge...She fled as an immigrant to a foreign country, and without proper papers, in order to keep her Child safe...La Madre Grande is a force of Nature intrinsically inlaid with the profound creativity- of bringing, teaching, showing, sheltering, all the attributes of mothering in this world and beyond...As vast intercessor, she is essential to *Tikkun Olam,* the Hebraic words meaning 'repair of the soul of the world.' She is essential to the concept of *Ometeotl,* the Nahuatl/Aztec word meaning 'the one who

---

112 Ibid. pp.275/276

enters the world from highest heaven to sweep clear the two-way path between the great earthly and heavenly hearts once again.'"[113]

We need Mary's friendship and gentle encouragement.

So much of what I've written thus far has been in patriarchal language...as you have likely noticed. That's the world I grew up in. It was male rulers, falsely claiming to be acting under the authority of Christ, who launched the catastrophic wars in the wake of which we all still stumble. Would young women have obeyed orders to massacre one another as readily as young men did?

May the Blessed Mother soften our suspicious sceptical unyielding hearts...because there are reflexes, left over from our time in the jungle, that still tell us to fear neighbours as aliens, not love them as parts of ourselves.

Long ago I was a tiny cog in the mighty machine of London news. Everything in that feverish world revolved round a small geographical area known as Fleet Street. Rumours flowed up and down the street...you could almost see them, a swarm, a murmuration, never ceasing. Young men running from one office or pub to another, "Have you heard?"

That solid, agitated world has vanished like a dream... but the murmurations go on, more than ever before, not confined to a few streets but everywhere, every second of every minute of every day, on screens, through headphones and in our pockets. Rumours! Breaking news! Instant reaction to instant reaction! Are you one of us?

Or are you a foe: to be feared, ridiculed... spat on?

---

113 Clarissa Pinkola Estes, Untie the Strong Woman, Sounds True, 2013, pp.188/189

When people meet, as opposed to shouting insults on electronic media, they are sometimes surprised by the complex human reality they encounter, utterly different from keyboard braggadocio. Similarly, when former combatants met after the satanic wars, they were often moved by what they had in common.

Empathy. That's one vital key that will unlock the future, here on this little planet.

But to achieve empathy...to love our neighbours as ourselves... we need an evolutionary re-boot. How might that be accomplished?

One of the gifts we acquired in our original homeland (along with reflexes of fear) was an ability to listen. We evolved complex ears, and we listen of course through our eyes and other animal senses, as well as with soul and psychic attributes.

To those innate abilities have been added, especially in the twentieth century, ground-breaking psychological insights. You or I may not claim particular expertise in such matters; but we can be taught to listen, or at the very least, not to be continually interrupting.

Genuine openness to the witness of another, not treating conversation as a contest I must win: surely that's the aspiration of loving my neighbour as myself made, for a few moments, real.

Unfortunately I am a mediocre listener. But at the beginning and again towards the end of my church career I was fortunate to meet teachers who had been disciples of Carl Rogers, founder of "person-centred" therapy.

Rogers had taught three "Core Conditions" for satisfactory listening. The first of them, congruence, is about genuineness, "...without facade and without any attempt to assume or hide behind a...role. Such congruence...is dependent upon...a high level of self-awareness."[114] That was, and remains, creatively challenging for "religious" actors such as myself, who are expected to represent traditional fixed points of reference amid the flow of life.

However, the second of Rogers' "Core Conditions" came more easily: acceptance, "...an outgoing positive feeling without reservations, without evaluations. The term we have come to use for this is unconditional personal regard."[115] What a contrast to the criticizing views that had surrounded me, most of my life! No requirements to earn approval, no need to fit in with values and prejudices of the tribe: you are accepted...just as you are.

That is what I have experienced all along in the divine: deep, patient acceptance...before all else.

Rogers, who was not a religious man, took an optimistic view of the potential for human flourishing. Such an "actualizing tendency" as he called it, "...may become deeply buried under layer after layer of encrusted psychological defences; it may be hidden behind elaborate facades which deny its existence; it is my belief, however, that it exists in every individual, and awaits only the proper conditions to be released and expressed."[116]

Needless to say, such a positive view was heavily criticized in his own time as naive. Christians said Rogers failed to take "original sin" into account, Freudians accused him of ignoring the cavern of the unconscious and behaviourists complained his theories paid little attention to the all-important outward circumstances of existence.

---

114 Brian Thorne, Carl Rogers, Sage Publications, 1992, pp.36/37
115 Carl Rogers, On Becoming a Person, Constable & Robinson, 1961, p.62
116 Ibid., p.351

I have recently seen his work dismissed by a Catholic historian as a "farrago of uplift."[117]

Such rebuttals may, for all I know, have their plausibility. The "person centred" way of counselling developed by Rogers has certainly been effective in restoring wholeness to many, and remains an influence for good in our dark and dangerous world. But any method of doing anything will have its critics; and I am not qualified to enter into arguments about forms of therapy.

What I am qualified to say is that in my ordinary, everyday life Carl Rogers' theories, since I first heard about them as a young adult, have been a continuous source of challenge and encouragement. They have reminded me, on a day-to-day basis, to give attention, not just as some kind of pastor but as a person. To do so, I have had to try to listen to myself as well as to the other. Especially as a male cleric, the assertion of "status" and position was a pestilent hole into which it was all too easy to slide. Evaluation and judgement, irritation and boredom: "Stay awake" said Jesus (often irritated by his own disciples, according to the gospel accounts), notice those reactions but don't let yourself get sucked in. Remember, at all times, that the other (whatever you feel about him or her) is a child of God.

To give full attention, unconditionally, is the greatest gift we can give another human being.

Easy to write, endlessly difficult to do.

But Carl Rogers has long been a source of encouragement for me as well as challenge. The third of his "Core Conditions" was empathy, about which he wrote "...we have in our hands, if we are able to take an empathic stance, a

---

117 Eugene McCarraher, The Enchantments of Mammon, Belknap, 2019, p.553

powerful force for change and growth. Its strength needs to be appreciated."[118]

I have found that an understatement. Humanly, empathy is almost miraculous in its transformative power. It's the gentle mother, holding open the lion's jaws.

Empathy has been in short supply, however, in the concrete catacomb of name-calling, knee-jerk reactions and tribal team-calls that electronic communication has become here in England during my lifetime.

We must evolve.

Maybe that can only happen person by person, each of us doing what we can. "Before you speak of peace" St Francis said long ago, to his original friars, "you must first have it in your heart...We have been called to heal wounds, to unite what has fallen apart, and to bring home any who have lost their way."[119]

It's easy to see how all of the above can be mocked, along with Christ himself, as naive. Well, so be it!

Etty Hillesum gave unconditional personal regard to men whose hearts, souls, minds and strength had been possessed by Nazism. The sensible path would have been to despise them, but she understood that as a road to nowhere. Jesus forgave Caiaphas and Pilate and the soldiers who nailed him to a cross: and by doing so showed the circle of life as not a windowless prison but an open, upward spiral through which astonishing sunlight sometimes shines.

To love, to recognise I Am in the other, to say Namaste to my neighbour no matter in what evil he may presently be engaged: unacceptable? ridiculous?

---

118 Carl Rogers, A Way of Being, Houghton Mifflin, 1980, pp.159/160
119 Quoted in Richard Rohr, The Wisdom Pattern, Franciscan Media, 2020, p.1

Yet around the world love goes quietly about its business, while tsunamis of hatred and judgement rage. The lady gently holds the lion's jaws. The lion is content to let his jaws be held.

Such empathy, such holy naivety conceals within it a possible rumour: that this life isn't all.

There's another, higher crossbeam. In the sketch I'm using it indicates further frequencies for which our crazy empathy might be preparation. "In my Father's house there are many dwelling places" (John 14:2).

To those rumoured realms I now turn.

NINETEEN

Love your neighbour (iii)

There are worlds aplenty of which you and I know little. The ocean depths of our planet, and their inhabitants, are one such region. The teeming interiors of your and my guts might be another.

All my life there has been speculation about the possibilities of life elsewhere in the physical universe. By the time you are reading this, for all I know contact may have been made with so-called "aliens."

But there are rumoured to be other dimensions of existence beyond what may be observed through telescopes or microscopes. Such rumours reach back into ancient history, and are enshrined in the liturgies of the world's religions. For instance, in one of the Jewish titles of God carried over into Christianity, "Lord of Hosts", the divinity is pictured surrounded by shoals of "Angels and Archangels and all the company of heaven."[120]

Some of these reputed non-material dimensions are within and part of the life of our planet. For instance, many people experience communication with trees and natural phenomena[121], or describe electronic gadgetry weirdly

---

120 (These words are recited in the preface to the Eucharistic Prayer of many traditional Christian churches.)

121 See, for instance, Stephanie Kaza, Conversations with Trees, 2019

manipulated[122]. Such enigmas may encourage a sense of all inhabitants of earth being in some degree conscious, the "panpsychism" spoken of earlier.

But alleged experiences also suggest energies powerful as radio and television waves coming from extra-terrestrial parts of the cosmos: the many-dimensioned "post-mortem" realms, for instance, including saints and bodhisattvas but also every variety of human who has ever lived. Others might emanate from mysterious orders of life called (by us) "angelic" or "devic."

We are grains of sand in creation, limited by our specific location in a particular world in a limited dimension at a certain time. "In my Father's house" Jesus states laconically "there are many dwelling places" (John 14:2). Traces of some of those other dwelling places may entangle themselves with our everyday existence.

The third horizontal bar on our imaginary cross, head-high, represents our invisible neighbours in purported subtle and spiritual realms. It isn't possible even to attempt the beginnings of a map of such territories; and the point of this entire essay is to promote love, not merely to speculate.

So rather than blunder onwards into the more or less unknown, what I propose doing is use a ubiquitous Christian prayer, the "Our Father," as a template to help us look at just a tiny corner of this infinitely vast and complex subject.

"Our Father in heaven:"[123] the first word to remember is "our." If the one to whom the prayer is addressed is

---

122 See, for instance, David Spangler, Techno-Elementals, Lorian, 2012
123 The "Lord's Prayer" is in Matthew 6:9–13 and, slightly differently, Luke 11:2–4

considered my father, "he" is also everybody else's, including creatures of all realms, human, non-human and extra-human. That makes us all brothers and sisters (and whatever genders may be elsewhere), owing one another the allegiance, friendliness and love of siblings.

So if, in some cosmic exploration, I come across a being unknown, a stranger to earth and her children, that creature, for all its strangeness to me, is still the child of my "father" and thus a relative of mine, to be approached with respect, not terror.

The "father" of course is not a giant human. The word is a figure of speech, simply meant to reassure us about our relatedness to "him."

As to "in heaven", we may try to picture how that would be. Artists have often attempted to do so. The word simply refers to our origin. Heaven is the state from which all we know and don't know springs: where "God's will" is done. Imagine, in words or images or music or some other way: how might heaven be, for you?

Heaven really is. Whatever catastrophes may occur "here below", heaven is: nothing can take that away.

It would be interesting to find out how heaven is imagined in other parts of the cosmos.

When Jesus was hanging on the cross, he said to the remorseful criminal nailed next to him, "Truly I tell you, today you will be with me in Paradise"(Luke 23:43). We like to imagine our loved ones arriving in a beautiful environment after they die: 'Paradise' is an Iranian concept in which that desired state is pictured as a garden. Muslim horticulturalists have striven to create paradise gardens that put people in mind of heaven.

"Hallowed be your name": but we don't know what God's name is. A name is a human handle by which to get hold of someone. As mentioned above, thousands of

supposed names are given for the Holy One here on earth.
Each in its limited way may be a threshold to presence.

For us a name is usually the first we get to hear about
the sacred. That name might be God or Allah, or Brahman,
it might be Jesus or Spirit, or it might be the four unspoken
Hebrew letters sometimes roughly done into English as
"Yahweh" or "Jehovah" or "I Am."

In heaven we're told they don't bother with names or
have any need of them. The Holy One can be imagined
surrounded by limitless beings who know the actual reality.

Then there are all the others, like us, who still need
names as handholds. The picture given by this phrase in
the Lord's Prayer is of the Holy One not austerely isolated,
but continuously "hallowed", connecting with a vast halo
of beings, encircled with praise and joy.

Among that ring of lovers, changing day to day, will be
creatures from orders loosely described as "angelic." The
Bible word has to do with message-bearing; in the Hebrew
scriptures those angel-lieutenants were so closely identified
with their creator that each sometimes seemed to merge
with the other.[124]

The same can be true now. Creatures known as angels
are quite widely recognized among my supposedly-materi-
alistic contemporaries. They are spoken of as emissaries
from on high, conduits of blessing, even (as mentioned
earlier) by people who admit little interest otherwise in
the life of the soul.

"We can only recognize other beings" wrote alchemist
Catherine MacCoun "to the extent that we have something
in common with them, for we experience them at the

124e.g. Genesis 16: 7–13, Exodus 3:2–4.

point where their consciousness overlaps our own."[125] Thus we might encounter angels, creatures of connection, at moments when we recognize our need of heaven, even if that need is fleeting or has to do with entirely mundane matters.

I was told from an early age I had someone called a guardian angel watching over me. Jesus had said, "Take care that you do not despise one of these little ones; for, I tell you, in heaven their angels continually see the face of my Father in heaven"(Matthew 18:10). I would have hated the thought of being "watched over" at certain times in my life. No member of the angelic clan will barge in completely uninvited.

But there were moments, nonetheless, when "heaven" seemed to take a view, give a shove, and possibly pull a lever or two. Something in my soul must have resonated at those times with whatever "sacred contract" my angelic friend was there to encourage.

Lately I've had a clearer sense of the reality of this courteous, patient creature: light in both senses, infinitely agile, ageless and sexless, not as portrayed in church windows but showing (to me) non-human appearance, ceaselessly available, willing to protect, a two-way envoy for such prayers and inspirations as may sometimes flow between me and the realm called heaven.

"Your kingdom come. Your will be done, on earth as it is in heaven." Words such as "kingdom" and "Lord" were used by people of a particular time and place to speak of unspeakable realities. They used the highest terms of honour they could find, aware such words were paltry

---

125 Catherine MacCoun, On Becoming an Alchemist, Trumpeter, 2008, p.94

figures of speech. Unfortunately religious use has had the effect of turning poetry into authorized jargon.

The "Kingdom of Heaven" describes a state in which the "will" of God is fulfilled and accomplished. The point of the phrase "Your kingdom come" is to align our wishes with the wholeness known in heaven but not yet anywhere else.

We and all beings are work in progress, evolving. That applies to saints and bodhisattvas too, and maybe angels and devas. How could there yet be finality or completion?

Certainly not in our earth realm and its environs. Think of your deceased relatives, or even of supposedly saintly figures. However well they lived their lives, each was limited by time and circumstances and genetics. In order to realise the gifts within them, they must evolve. And so must you and I.

We are free to develop in whatever way. In Bible mythology, the initial act of supposed misdirection came from a "crafty" talking serpent (Genesis 3:1), who lured Eve and then Adam into eating magic fruit, so that "the eyes of both were opened, and they knew that they were naked... "(Genesis 3:7) That very release into freedom is portrayed as rebellion against God. Yet only the free can truly love.

The prayer includes an aspiration that God's will might be done "on earth." The "Hanged Man" Tarot card shows its subject suspended upside down by one ankle from a horizontal bar or tree-branch. Despite his posture, the "Hanged Man" looks blissfully happy. The card appears to portray alignment of our earthly wishes with those of heaven...it's a sketch of our precarious, ongoing evolution.

"The Hanged Man" writes Valentin Tomberg "represents the condition of one in the life of whom gravitation from above has replaced that from below."[126] "Very truly I tell

---

126 Meditations on the Tarot, p.307

you" Jesus said to Nicodemus, "no-one can see the kingdom of God without being born from above" (John 3:3).

Jesus' public work, according to St Mark, began with the exhortation "...the kingdom of God has come near, repent and believe in the good news" (Mark 1:15). Old time Christian religion went a bit overboard on repentance, often mixed with ladlefuls of shame.

However, the Bible word conventionally done into English as "repentance"[127] can equally well be translated, as Cynthia Bourgeault has argued, "go beyond the mind" or "into the larger mind." "This is" writes Bourgeault "the central message of Jesus. This is what this Kingdom of Heaven is all about. 'Let's get into the larger mind...This is what it looks like. This is how you do it. Here, I'll help you...'"[128]

Knowing "God's will" as sunshine and pointing ourselves in its direction unshutters our closed windowless hearts and allows everything to grow. It requires we love God and neighbour: which might at first feel as difficult as hanging upside down by one leg. Hence "repent and believe," "go into the larger mind."

"Give us this day our daily bread": again, the key word, as preachers down the centuries have pointed out, is "us". In every way, the teaching of Jesus and other sages reminds us that the practice of love, here and throughout the cosmos, is the key that unlocks all doors. In famous, much-quoted words, St Paul wrote that "Love never ends...And now faith, hope and love abide, these three; and the greatest of these is love."(I Corinthians 13: 8, 13)

And yet we know how easy it is to recite those words, how hard it can be to perform them. On a railway bridge

---

127 (Metanoia)
128 Cynthia Bourgeault, The Wisdom Jesus, Shambala, 2008, p.41

in the first parish where I worked, someone had painted in big letters NO SUPPER NO JUSTICE TONIGHT.[129] That may have been true for some of the parishioners in that place at that time, and you'll be able to think of many for whom it's certainly true now.

"Daily bread" obviously means what it says, physical sustenance, but it also refers to what keeps us alive in other ways: dignity, inspiration, hope. If I recite the Lord's Prayer, I am asking for "us" not "me", and the love involved isn't some sentimental mush, but the actuality of ensuring "we" (not just I) can flourish.

That is where I expect my fancy words about co-creating a world where love prevails to face proper interrogation. What am I doing, saying and thinking that depletes my neighbours? Never mind "give us our daily bread", in what ways have I taken "daily bread" away from others? Maybe I didn't mean to, maybe it's the way of living I inherited along with language and much else.

It might not have occurred to my eighteenth-century ancestors that the slave-owning society they were part of was based on a shameful evil, as now seems obvious to us. Opinions about "justice" evolve: what we observe through the rear mirror is often strikingly different from what was seen at the time; and through it all, and through us all without exception (be we ever so righteous in our own eyes) runs the "crack" some Jews call "the breaking of the vessels" and some Christians call "original sin."

Thus, probably the best I can do is live kindly, while accepting I will often mess up.

Post-mortem, in the expectation of many religious people and more recently in accounts of "Near Death Experiences"

---

129 (Probably based on the song Armagideon Time, by The Clash)

there is a judgement, sometimes gently referred to as a "Life Review." "Everything you have done is there in the review for you to evaluate (and) when I was there in that review there was no covering up. I was the very people that I hurt, and I was the very people I helped..."[130]

We may expect that awesome procedure to be administered with extra-human all-seeing wisdom and compassion. That is where those beings we refer to as angels may come into their own, helping to administer the luminous divine will.

But "...with the judgement you make you will be judged" according to Jesus, "and the measure you give will be the measure you get. Why do you see the speck in your neighbour's eye, but do not notice the log in your own eye?"(Matthew 7: 2, 3)

Which leads to one of the most powerful and troubling phrases in this famous prayer: "And forgive us our debts, as we also have forgiven our debtors." How easy it is to preach about forgiveness! How complex and hazardous the reality!

Once again, the key word is "us." We are all involved in this, collectively as well as individually, our clans and ranks as well as our own little souls.

I am part of a nation, the English, who have stomped their hobnailed boots throughout the world, uprooting here, exploiting there. Witness the hegemony of the English language...it didn't come about through gentle scholarly exchanges. Does that fact poison my soul?

But even more diminishing has been the thoughtlessness with which I have often inflicted harm on others. Any encounter with a being of light is likely to expose that miserable rottenness.

---

130 Quoted in Kenneth Ring, Lessons from the Light, Moment Point Press, 2000, p.159

There is (fortunately) a real presence embedded in wayward creation. In a context of human counselling, it was named by (agnostic) Carl Rogers "the actualizing tendency"; it animates all beings, presumably in every dimension, to move towards their own "Congruence, or genuineness."[131]

Identified at different times and called by different names (such as Tao), this presence could be seen as the originating mystery working among and within us[132]. ("Where is God?" the nun enquired. "God is everywhere" we children chanted back. "Tzimtzum," according to some at least of its Jewish proponents, is a story not of absence but concealment).[133]

Yet, according to Carl Rogers, the actualizing tendency "can...be stunted or stopped altogether. Sometimes, too, it is only able to exert itself in 'warped, bizarre or abnormal manifestations; and turns in socially destructive ways rather than constructive ways.'"[134]That's why in Christian prayers we plead continually for help from the Holy Spirit, that "blows where it chooses, and you hear the sound of it, but you do not know where it comes from or where it goes" (John 3:8).

Assistance may also come through angels, messengers of divine grace. And formerly incarnate humans may help if asked, shining their more homely light into murky regions of our souls. They may be people acknowledged as "saints" in mainstream religions, though I guess there are many

---

131 Carl Rogers, A Way of Being, p.160
132 (See Luke 17:21. The Greek word used by Luke can be translated "within" or "among.")
133 See Zalman Schacter-Shalomi and Netanel Miles-Yepez, God Hidden, 2013, pp.23–24
134 Brian Thorne, Carl Rogers, p.27

more such luminous souls in contact with earth than are known by churches or temples.

I mention those, probably quaint-sounding traditional beliefs... at certain times I would have gone along with materialistic consumerism and ignored them...because they seem to me to work, sometimes startlingly well. They reassure us we are not alone. Existence is not just an "indifferent immensity". There are friends surprisingly near we can call on.

But, as soon as we do: they'll see us naked. They are likely to be unimpressed by whatever titles or achievements we try to hide behind.

So the "Life Review" has to begin now.

That won't be a pretty sight in the short term. Maybe our missteps are small. But we'll have to face who we are at present, what we've done, failed to do. Accessing divine grace requires self-knowledge. "Blessed are the poor in spirit"(Matthew 5:3) said Jesus at the very start of his Sermon on the Mount. Bragging isn't going to impress heaven[135].

Then, maybe there are actions we regret very much indeed. Perhaps they can't be undone, and humanly they can't be healed.

However, "As a handful of sand thrown into the ocean, so are the sins of all flesh as compared with the mind of God."[136]

Fully acknowledging that reality for ourselves can be breathtaking.

It also makes it more possible we will forgive others. Self-awareness enables us, sometimes, to hang upside down by one leg. And smile.

---

135 (See Luke 18: 9–14)
136 St Isaac of Syria, in A.M.Allchin, ed., Heart of Compassion, Darton, Longman and Todd, 1989, p.37

(I don't, however, underestimate how exceedingly difficult the task of forgiveness might be. Sometimes, especially where an offender seems oblivious, the best we can aim for is: acknowledge the ultimate rightness of forgiveness, hand the offence, whatever it is, to God, and don't actively seek revenge.)

I want to conclude these few inadequate words about forgiveness, a vital subject on which many wise people have spoken[137], by repeating: we are not alone. When faced with tragic or challenging circumstances, in addition to our all-important friends and family members, there are subtle helpers on whom we may wish to call.

Which leads into the darkest depths of this prayer: "Do not bring us to the time of trial, but rescue us from the evil one."

People have sometimes approached me after a church service to express concern about those words, especially in the traditional form "Lead us not into temptation." How can God, supposedly good, induce "temptation"?

My reply has usually been, we know life is an improvisation, not fully scripted, and we know the characters evolve. So as the play goes on, circumstances will arise that test us. How we handle those crises will affect the way we grow...or fail to.

"The time of trial" suggests a particularly harrowing ordeal: maybe in everyone's life there is one happening above all that is formative. In the prayer, we plead to be spared anything too drastic: however, we know the originating mystery does allow people into times and places of great moral and physical danger. How has that played out in your life?

---

137 E.g Desmond and Mpho Tutu, The Book of Forgiving, Harper Collins, 2015

In the gospel, after Jesus' baptism "the Spirit immediately drove him out into the wilderness. He was in the wilderness forty days, tempted by Satan; and he was with the wild beasts; and the angels waited on him" (Mark 1: 12, 13).

The Holy Spirit, referred to in John's gospel by the reassuring title "Advocate" or "Comforter," is also bracingly called (in the next breath) "Spirit of truth"(John 14: 16,17). That Spirit may lead even little us through tests and conflicts, maybe wildernesses in the middle of which we find out who we are and what it is we're supposed to be doing.

So what about the "evil one" from whom we ask to be rescued?

Many Christians and others seem fascinated by thoughts of Satan and the demonic hordes. It has long been a custom of religions reaching back into antiquity to presume a single personalized fulcrum of depravity, and such a picture (used by Jesus and the evangelists) may help us recognize hard evil and steer well clear of it. I find it difficult myself to imagine "evil" obeying anything, let alone commands from a single demigod, so I picture instead conflicting swarms of beings, sometimes cynically allied, mostly at war with themselves and everyone else. That's just my story, to set alongside all the others.

What matters, however, is not this or that myth, but how "evil" impacts on us right now. What is it we are asking to be delivered from?

I mentioned so-called egregores, collective thought-forms that take on lives of their own. Not all are harmful; some are just patterns of habit, others may even be narrowly constructive.

But sometimes a thought-form possessing a number of minds seems itself controlled by some stranger and more toxic entity. The golden rule of discernment here is "You will know them by their fruits" (Matthew 7:16). Results incompatible with divine mercy and love are (especially if they claim the name of God) deceptions pure and simple.

On a more personal level, it's alleged by those with knowledge of such matters that deceased but earthbound souls sometimes try to insinuate themselves through vulnerable humans. For instance, "A man who has a habit of anger...is certain to be surrounded by antagonistic spirits. I have seen a score of them around a man, thrilling him with their own malignant magnetism..."[138]

In my world as maybe yours it would be usual to dismiss such ideas as gothic fantasies. We presume everything within us is self-generated.

However, I believe we are complex, amphibious creatures, embodied, ensouled, with fabulous root systems and porous, hazy boundaries. Often what ails us may be identified, ministered to, at least given a name. But not always. The vertical and lateral roots of our human lives and souls are far-reaching and tangled. Sometimes in my parishes I visited sorrowing people no psychiatry could reach. All I could offer was unconditional regard...along with prayer, if the person was willing to be prayed for.

In Brazil, "Spiritists" run certain respected mental health facilities. They claim "obsession" of living people by deceased spirits can be a factor in inner disorder, alongside more familiar causes. "These harmful influences can happen when an obsessing spirit exacerbates negative thoughts and feelings in the patient through a kind of telepathy."[139]

I think it regrettable we in the "enlightened" north are

---

138 Judge David Patterson Hatch, quoted in Stafford Betty, 2014,p.124
139 Emma Bragdon, ed., Spiritism and Mental Health, Singing Dragon, 2012, p.40

obliged to deny such possibility. Just as there are friends and helpers on the other side of the veil, so there might be subtle opponents. Anyone who prays intently might occasionally feel themselves under attack, showered with a hail of (usually not very effective) missiles. It's normally easy to smile at such nonsense.

But sometimes the attacks might get more serious, especially if we are vulnerable or depleted. The Psalms of ancient Israel seem to speak of such harassment. "Why must I walk about mournfully because the enemy oppresses me? As with a deadly wound in my body, my adversaries taunt me, while they say to me continually, 'Where is your God?'"(Psalm 42: 9, 10).

Again, you might encounter some person guilty of grievous wrongdoing. You won't be able to recognise him by horns and forked tail. Quite likely, he may smile and behave in a way that seems plausible and attractive. Perhaps he has been or is being horribly deceived himself.

"When we do evil" wrote Simone Weil "we do not know it, because evil flies from the light."[140] How can such catastrophes come about?

Any of us is capable of being swamped, by the times we live in, by our own needs and desires, through the influence of others. Such others might, or might not, be embodied. Sometimes we only begin to understand long after the event, through the rear mirror.

Invisible enemies are likely crafty, sophisticated and tenacious, even if ultimately, according to Simone Weil, "gloomy, monotonous, barren, boring."[141] Self-awareness

---

140 Simone Weil, trs. Emma Crawford and Mario von der Ruhr, Gravity and Grace, Routledge and Kegan Paul, 1952, p.71
141 Ibid., p.70

gives us some protection, and so, very definitely, does prayer.

But there is "a crack, a crack through everything": even through you and me.

We can, of course, perfectly well understand injustice and cruelty on earth, and ask to be delivered from them, without having to venture into psychic shadow lands. We are more than capable of behaving badly without help from outside.

In order not to be part of the "evil" someone else needs deliverance from, however, I must try to live kindly...love my neighbour. In whatever way we think of it, "Jihad Akbar," the struggle to go into the larger mind, to reach for the sun, continues, every day of our lives: it does for me, anyway.

Let me end by offering a story of divine love in a post-mortem environment.

Frances Banks was an Anglican nun, esteemed as an educator. She died in the mid-twentieth century. Not long after her passing, an old and close friend, Helen Greaves, became certain Frances was trying to communicate. "Words dropped into my thoughts, which did not come from my consciousness."[142] Something about the words rang bells. So Helen began to write them down.

What followed was a series of descriptions purporting to be of some nearer reaches of the human post-mortem realms, inhabited by individuals not long physically dead. Among them was one described by Frances as a "patient": "The man had been a Nazi leader; well-known and extremely powerful during the last war. After the downfall

---

142 Helen Greaves, *Testimony of Light*, Penguin, 1969, p.6

of Germany he had committed suicide...Since that time he had been 'lodged in the shadows'...'wandering in the lower places'...imprisoned by his own evil...Now he had been rescued. He was conscious of his terrible cruelty and filled with remorse...The ward was dark and gloomy...Only slowly did it become apparent to us that 'something' lay on the bed...The man was a terrible and pathetic sight...'He has come to us to be healed and to be enabled to face himself and judge his deeds when he wakens from his terrible ordeal of darkness...Let us ask that Light may come into this place'..."[143]

What that little scene offers is a picture of a human being who has inflicted grievous suffering and has arrived at a low point of degradation. Yet something has been kindled, what we might call "the self-actualizing tendency" has begun, even in the most miserable depths, to stir; and, crucially, love has not given up, even on one so seemingly corrupted.

"Lead us not into temptation. Deliver us from evil."

---

143 Ibid., pp. 40, 41

TWENTY

...as yourself

You didn't ask to be born, and nor did I. But here we are.

The place I landed was peaceable, though noisy. There was continuous tread of traffic from the main road nearby. Shunting engines were clattering trucks in a rail yard a few streets away, their steam visible above the rooftops. Propeller powered aircraft passed low overhead. At night there were often alluring voices of young adults out on the green close to our house, chattering, laughing. "Teddy boys", Mum said, mysteriously.

For whatever reason, I grew up considering myself an outsider. I was cack-handed at sport, and unlikely to be part of anyone's gang. I would have loved to have joined the voices on the green, but that was never going to happen. The Catholic boys' school to which I was sentenced at eleven taught me little other than how to survive, and supplied me with nightmares well into adulthood.

"You are a person" pronounced would-be-Freudian art tutor Jonathan, when at last I'd escaped to art school, "who is afraid of people." That judgement stuck in my throat. But he was probably right.

It's ironic how the preacher in me has held forth about the all-importance of love, considering how neglectful and ignorant that preacher has usually been about love when not in his pulpit. The crack that runs through everything: there's a long list of folk to whom I owe apologies, from today stretching right back to childhood. "Fool" in the title of these chapters very definitely describes the person who has written them.

But "The Fool" is also the title of a Tarot card. It portrays a young man moseying dreamily along the edge of a cliff. "He is like the child discovering life for the first time, or the adult searching for a new meaning or sense of purpose. The Fool seeks the truth, and turns his attention towards the spirit in search of truth. His madness or foolishness links him to the divine, for originally the word 'silly' meant 'blessed'..."[144]

This un-asked-for life has been an adventure, sometimes agreeable. One of Jesus' instructions to his disciples was that they "take up their cross and follow me" (Matthew 16:24). That "cross" is different for each of us. To me, the cross I have most struggled to bear has been my own faulty nature.

But "Who told you that you were naked?"(Genesis 3:11)

The price we pay for our freedom is the brilliance, stupidity and scope for wonder and disaster that makes this un-asked-for life the improvisation it is. Christ's outstretched arms on the cross promise divine forbearance, which is why we put crosses on graves and wear them on earrings and necklaces.

When I remember the stupendous truth that heaven disregards my clownishness and that today is a new day, I also see: the same goes for everybody else.

If you, God, had wanted a predictable cosmos where everyone obeyed orders, you could surely have made it.

I seem to be tolerated. My neighbours in their diversity and varying degrees of probity are also allowed. We are inescapably creatures of the same origin.

---

144 Juliet Sharman-Burke, The Complete Book of Tarot, Pan, 1985, p.27

Therefore me bearing grudges or striking judgemental poses is futile, just "An-Nafs-al-Ammarah."

My neighbours and I are kindred. We need to put up with being sisters and brothers (and whatever other sexes there may be in the cosmos), arguing and competing, yes, but ultimately family. No-one has ever said that would be easy or straightforward.

But to seek the best for my neighbour, to be grounded in unconditional positive regard, is to be at peace with my own roots, including the many horizontal ones. To honour my neighbour is to be "born from above" (John 3:3) and to become truly myself. It seems to me the sooner we discover that, and act on it, the better.

However, it will not only seem difficult but nonsense, if we disregard any idea of divinity and accept the secular myth of radical aloneness.

"Living in a disenchanted world" philosopher Charles Taylor wrote, "the buffered self is no longer open, vulnerable to a world of spirits and forces which cross the boundary of the mind, indeed, negate the very idea of there being a boundary...This sense of self-possession, of a secure inner mental realm, is all the stronger, if in addition to disenchanting the world, we have also taken the anthropocentric turn, and no longer even draw on the power of God"[145].

It won't be necessary to say by now that I am an unbeliever in that bracing secular faith. We may not any longer be willing to accept confinement in antique religious cages. But adult liberty won for us by philosophers and scientists doesn't have to indicate an indifferent universe.

This is what my corner of the cosmos feels like to me, at this moment:

---

145 Charles Taylor, 2007, pp.300, 301

On the one hand: we are entangled with "macro" cultures and traditions within which we emerge into the light of day. For me that was welfare-state suburban England in the immediate aftermath of world conflict: smoking chimneys, shabby streets, steam engines, motor vehicles, endless talk about "the war." My whole life has played out within a commercial consumerist egregore so irresistibly powerful it is not generally seen as a specific belief-system but just "how things are."

On the other hand: even in our bodies we know genetic "recombination" makes each of us unique, not merely a "consumer" or statistic.

People entangle with us, change us (as allegedly do beings from other frequencies). Some of those entanglements may be chance encounters. A few might turn out to be toxic or even, tragically, murderous.

But the miserablest and most despotic harm can sometimes, in the very long run, be transposed into radiance (not without great struggle) through openness to originating grace.

Jesus' resurrection appearances to his amazed friends included, disturbingly, showing them his wounds (John 20: 20, 27). Those wounds became, in the imagination of many, not marks of shame but wellsprings of healing and hope.

I have known others who in smaller ways have achieved comparable alchemy; maybe you have.

You may also have knowledge of your own inner configuration: your soul.

In England during my lifetime, those who suspected they were souls and not mere consumers increasingly shunned conventional religion. They sought, instead, "spirituality:" a path not proscribed by any institution or belief-system.

Christians, secularists and others were often quick to

ridicule such free-range vision quests as egoistical and flaky.

But at its best "spirituality" refuses to be hemmed in, either by authoritarian "God Said" or reductive "Nothing But". It's The Fool, willing to mosey along a cliff edge or hang upside down by one foot, blissfully unconcerned what any system, religious or otherwise, thinks of him.

Variegated "spirituality" may seem to have no creeds or structure; but its very individualism, its emphasis on personal authenticity, is itself a shared belief, from which people can and do network and create shifting alliances.

"My Way" nearly always becomes transpersonal in practice; no-one can go it alone. It's also usually interspiritual. Acupuncturists read tarot cards. Yoga teachers study the Kabbalah. Crystal healers walk labyrinths. Clairvoyants go for reflexology. Pagan witches believe in reincarnation.

That may not seem a religious environment as conventionally understood; but it is a milieu, fed by popular culture, films, music, in which worlds collide and fertilize one another in unpredictable ways. Free-range spirituality in my lifetime has above all been playful, where traditional religious observance has often felt dreary.

The very qualities of improvisation and experiment that give this movement its élan, however, can also cause it to seem modish and shallow. Traditional faith still (at the time of writing) brings ordinary people together. What old religions might lack in flair and creativity, they sometimes make up for in heft.

Though friendly to other paths, I remain Christian (readers might disagree!) I have been lucky to live in times when religions that rooted and sustained people for centuries were suddenly next door to one another, their sacred writings freely available, first in paperback then online. That has provided wonderful opportunities for encounter.

Now it is almost normal for those in traditional churches, temples, synagogues to sample, like free-range seekers, practices and wisdom from clans other than their own. How could the origin of the cosmos be conceived to reside solely in One True Rightly-Guided corner, condemning everyone else to ignorance or lostness?

Towards the end of my time as an Anglican priest, I officiated at the funeral of a lady who had done much to help with the establishment of a Buddhist centre near where she and I lived. She had remained in her own eyes a faithful Anglican, while simultaneously practising Buddhism. She saw the two traditions as complementary, not contradictory. "She good Buddhist" said the Tibetan lama with whom I was privileged to share the church funeral, "and she good Christian!"

We have so much to share, so much with which to enrich one another! If we are to discover hope again after the satanic wars of the recent past, if we are to avoid poisoning and extinguishing this magical planet, we need to help one another reach for the sun. Love is at the heart of it.

"Yours, Lord, is the Kingdom, the power and the glory, for ever and ever. Amen." Those words conclude the Lord's Prayer as recited in Anglican churches. They are not part of what was taught by Jesus, but form a so-called "doxology"[146], a hymn to the known-yet-utterly-unknowable shape-shifter

---

146 (Based on David's prayer, 1 Chronicles 29:11)

who entangles with us, eludes and dances with us in limitless guises, to whom we sing by many names and whose heart connects uniquely with the spiritual heart of every one of us (the language may be figurative, but the reality is not).

In John's gospel we read that early in the morning after Jesus' execution, while it was still dark, Mary Magdalene went to his tomb and finding it opened and deserted, stood bewildered in the darkness, weeping...as many will be doing at this moment. It's always "all fuckin' shit" for some.

A male figure appeared nearby, whom she supposed to be a gardener. "Woman, why are you weeping?" he said, "Whom are you looking for?" She asked him if he knew where the corpse of Jesus had been taken.

In reply, he called to her by name: "Mary!" (John 20: 11, 14–16)

A few years ago, my stepson was digging a huge hole in his garden in order to make a fishpool. He had dug far down into primeval sands that had not seen sunlight for millennia.

I noticed a whitish stone down on the sand: it seemed to be beckoning to me.

With difficulty, I got down into the pit and picked up the oval-shaped stone. I must have been the first human ever to set eyes on it.

As I looked, I noticed it bore a small heart-shaped niche on one side, within which was a tiny perfect yellow heart, outlined in grey, with what resembled an aura of light radiating from it...just as on the "Sacred Heart" statue of Jesus in the church where Mum first took me to Mass all those years ago.

The stone lies on my desk as I write. I choose to consider

it the kindliest of epiphanies, a connection with loving presence glimpsed by my stony human heart: I Am, crucible of the cosmos.

Bibliography

Peter Ackroyd, London, The Biography, Vintage, 2001

A.M.Allchin, ed., Heart of Compassion, Darton Longman and Todd, 1989

Bernard Anderson, From Creation to New Creation, Fortress Press, 1994

Anon., trans.Patrick J.Gallacher, The Cloud of Unknowing, Western Michigan University, 1997

Anon.(Valentin Tomberg), trans. Robert Powell, Meditations on the Tarot, Tarcher/ Penguin, 1985

Sri Aurobindo, The Integral Yoga, Sri Aurobindo Ashram Trust, 1993

Ann Baring, The Dream of the Cosmos, Archive, 2013

John Barton, A History of the Bible, Allen Lane, 2019

Peter Berger, The Heretical Imperative, William Collins, 1979

Stafford Betty, Heaven and Hell Unveiled, White Crow Books, 2014

William Bloom, The Power of Modern Spirituality, Piatkus, 2011

Bonaventure, trans. Ewert Cousins, (various works), Paulist Press, 1978

Cynthia Bourgeault, The Wisdom Jesus, Shambala, 2008

Ian Bradley, God is Green, Darton Longman and Todd, 1990

Emma Bragdon, ed., Spiritism and Mental Health, Singing Dragon, 2012

Barbara Ann Brennan, Hands of Light, Bantam, 1985